T0043141

WISDOM FROM THE PSALMS

PETER KREEFT

WISDOM FROM THE PSALMS

IGNATIUS PRESS   SAN FRANCISCO

The King James Version of the Bible, which is quoted frequently in this book, uses italics to indicate words added by translators. These can be found in most printed and some online editions of the KJV, but are not being used in this book.

Cover art: Angel playing the harp
iStockphoto.com/aleroy4

Cover design by Riz Boncan Marsella

© 2020 by Ignatius Press, San Francisco
All rights reserved
ISBN 978-1-62164-344-9 (PB)
ISBN 978-1-64229-121-6 (eBook)
Library of Congress Catalogue number 2020933478
Printed in the United States of America ∞

CONTENTS

FOREWORD

Quite recently, when my friend Peter Kreeft was coming to town, I drove to Pittsburgh International Airport to pick him up. We sat down for coffee, as old friends do, and I reminded Peter that he had written the foreword for my first book, *Rome Sweet Home*. He smiled at the memory and said, "Then you'll have to write the foreword for my last." Well, I refused that assignment, but told him I'd gladly write one for his next.

So here I am, and here we are.

Peter hardly needs me as his herald. He has written a book for every one of his eighty-some years on the planet. He is a renowned philosopher and teacher of philosophy. He is the foremost living apologist for God's existence, and his work in this area has earned him a place with Newman and Pascal.

The man hardly needs a jeweler's kid from Pittsburgh to be his herald. But even if he doesn't need me (strictly speaking), it is certainly fitting for him to have a herald—because heralding is an important part of biblical religion, and it is nowhere so evident as in the subject of this book, the Book of the Psalms.

The Psalms are the most known and best-loved examples of biblical typology. Jesus quoted the Psalms more than any other book, and He considered them as anticipating and foreshadowing His own life and work. In the Psalms, the Savior was heralded by His own distinguished ancestor King David. All that was promised in the Psalms has been fulfilled in Jesus Christ and His Church.

The Psalms are something of a miracle. They are the words of Israel praying in David. They are the voice of Christ praying in the Church and the voice of the Church praying in Christ. It is a voice that contains the full range of human emotion and experience. Even after three thousand years, they remain (far more than the Beatles) "a voice that came from you and me".

No poems have had the staying power of the Psalms. The works of Homer and Vergil are studied today mostly as artifacts. Once the standard exercises of schoolchildren, they are today committed to memory by almost no one. Even Longfellow and Tennyson—the textbook poets of a century ago—are almost unknown to ordinary folks.

But the Psalms are still memorized. They are still taken to heart. And they still arise as prayers from the heart. Bluesmen wail their lines in the Mississippi Delta—and they mean every word. Congregations sing them in unison, and choirs sing them in harmony, and each and every member means the words in an intensely personal way.

The Psalms are, as we like to say, relevant. They always have been. They always will be. This is why the Church prays the Book of the Psalms twenty-four hours a day, seven days a week. The hermits of the Egyptian desert somehow managed to pray the entire book every single day! These are words that never get worn out. Committed to collective memory, they never become cliché. Nor do they become fossils to be admired in museums. After millennia, they are still living words. They are new, and they arrive as news.

I am tempted to say that, in all of this, they are a lot like Peter Kreeft, who has been around a long, long time and yet can still write books that exude a young man's vigor and joy. Not only that, he can still ride a surfboard better than almost any of us could in our teens.

But I have come to herald him, not to praise him or bury him. So I urge you to move now from promise to fulfillment and to admire the perennially youthful and always fresh craft of Kreeft.

INTRODUCTION

The Bible is the most well-known book in the world, and the Book of the Psalms is the most well-known, well-worn book in the Bible. Yet the Bible, and the Psalms in particular, are like the sea: they always have more unsuspected, surprising, and hidden depths to probe. This book's existence is justified only if it shows readers under-the-surface things that they have not seen before. Therefore, I have not consulted any other books or commentaries on the Psalms, because I did not want merely to repeat them, however valuable they are, but to say "Look!" anew. This is not a work of scholarship but one of midrash. (Look it up.)

🐝

The psalms are prayers. In every age, we need to learn anew how to pray, how to touch God as a plug touches a socket, as a candle touches a match, as a wire touches a dynamo. The disciples knew that; therefore, they asked Jesus, "Teach us to pray."

It is a plea—and, more, a demand—that we should be making of our clergy (but we are not making it) and one that all of them should be rigorously trained to answer (but they are not), parish priests as well as religious orders, and active orders as well as contemplative ones. How much of seminary training is directed to this absolutely essential personal umbilical cord with the God whose "business" we are all, in different ways, supposed to be in the "business" of doing? Instead, we are still clericalists: we let our priests and religious orders do the praying for us. Even less do we expect it of our bishops. All we expect from them is to be honest administrators, and we are continually crushingly disappointed even there. Even a pope can sometimes disappoint. Reform has to come from the bottom up. And you are at the bottom. That is why you are reading this book.

𝔅

When the disciples asked Jesus, "Teach us to pray", He did not give them any techniques, methods, yogas, or spiritual technologies. All the saints say that techniques, while often helpful, are not essential and are usually overemphasized. They say the same thing about feelings, our other modern obsession; and this also shocks us because we have divided our world into these two extremes, technology and feelings, and left everything important to fall through the enormous crack between the two.

This obsession with technique is especially popular today, when technology has become, not a secondary accident and accoutrement, but the essential force in our lives and, increasingly, in our thinking. But prayer is not a technology, not even a spiritual technology. Technology is a way of minimizing effort; prayer is a way of maximizing it. Technology is a way of thinking that uses matter more efficiently to satisfy our natural desires for power, pleasure, comfort, and security in this world. Prayer, by contrast, is not essentially a way of thinking but a way of loving. It uses thinking, reading, and speaking to change, not our world first of all, but our desires, our hearts, our loves; to habituate us to love God more and thus know God better, to care about lesser things less, and thus to understand them better (for addiction always blinds us), and thus to prepare us for the only life that satisfies our very deepest desire, the desire to share the very life of God.

What Jesus gave His disciples in answer to their request was, surprisingly, *words*, the words of "the Lord's Prayer". Those words are the architecture and the materials of a house: its form and its matter. In that house all of prayer lives. In that house of prayer is everything we need and, therefore, everything we need to pray for or to pray about. (Jesus included all four purposes of prayer—adoration, thanksgiving, and repentance as well as petition—but all in the form of petitions.) They are a little box that is bigger on the inside than on the outside. Indeed, what is in that box is bigger than the universe.

☙

Actually, Christ gave us not just one but four answers to the request "Teach us to pray."

First, he gave us "the Lord's Prayer", the prayer that contains all prayers because it contains everything we ought to pray for, everything we ought to love, everything we ought to hope for.

Second, He gave us His example. What prayers did He and His disciples pray? The Psalms! As all Jews have always done ever since they had them. The Psalms are *God's* answer to the request, "Teach us to pray." Christ prayed them not only in synagogue but throughout His life. He prayed Psalm 22, "My God, my God, why hast Thou forsaken me?" even as He was dying on the Cross.

Third, He gave us the Mass, the perfect prayer, in which we offer not just our prayers but our divine Pray-er Himself.

Fourth, He gave us His mother, from the Cross ("Woman, behold thy son ... Behold thy mother"). She is more than our example—she is our *mother!*—but she is also our example. Except for her *Magnificat*, Mary is almost totally silent in the Gospels. Her example of silent love, silent pondering, silent suffering, and silent adoration is for all of us, not just for monks and mystics.

Verbal prayers and wordless contemplative prayer are not an either-or. They are not rivals or choices: all of us need both. Most of us begin with verbal prayers and let them gently move us to more and more silent contemplation. The fundamental mistake most people make about contemplation, I think, is that they think it is purely mental, purely intellectual; and since most people are not "intellectuals", they classify it as something for philosophers, monks, and mystics. But the essence of contemplative prayer is not thought but love. Two lovers contemplating each other are not "intellectuals" who are trying to figure something out or get some new, creative, original ideas. They are just loving. That is all. That is what contemplative prayer is. Just be there and love Him and let Him love you. The Cure d'Ars' old peasant's is the best definition of contemplative prayer: "I just look at Him and He looks at me."

But the goodness of silent contemplative prayer does not mean that verbal prayers are not equally good, and necessary, at least to begin with. They are like the ground, and contemplative prayer is like the air, and planes need to begin with a runway on the ground in order to get into the air and fly.

Christ gave us a verbal prayer. He also prayed other verbal prayers. Some were spontaneous and original, but others were old and liturgical. We need both kinds. Christ's chief liturgical prayers were the Psalms. All Jews and Christians have used the Psalms, the prayer book God Himself provided for us. Because they are from God, they are like the Lord's Prayer in that they are far, far deeper and richer than they seem at first. They are like the sea.

This book is merely a sample and example of some ways to pray some psalms, some deep sea diving expeditions.

🐝

I use the old King James translation, first of all because it is a famous classic. Indeed, it is *the* primary classic in the English language. Every great English writer in history until the present century knew it and was influenced by it, even those who were non-Christian or anti-Christian.

But there are also three other even better reasons for using this translation: among Bible translations, it is one of the most beautiful, accurate, and powerful. I prefer it to many modern translations, especially most with the letter "N" (for "new") in them, because they sometimes edit the original in some "politically correct" ways such as using "inclusive" language—which is really exclusive language, since the old language used "man" inclusively to mean males and females equally, while the new so-called "inclusive" language insists that "man" does *not* include but excludes females, which was not the intention of the old writers at all. Thus it is not only politically skewed but also based on an inaccurate understanding of the intention of the original author. This is a cardinal sin for any translator, for the primary task for any honest translator is to tell you what the author actually said and meant, while many modern translators (especially those who use the philosophy of "dynamic equivalence") want to make it mean what they want it to mean and wish it meant. Even if that want and wish is for a good and noble goal, e.g.,

to end slavery or oppression or insensitivity or male chauvinism, it is simply not honest to insert oneself between
the author and the reader as if one were the co-author
or the author's editor and corrector. It is especially egre-
gious to try to edit the mail one believes is written (i.e.,
inspired) by God.

I write for Catholics and Protestants equally. Therefore, I use the KJV instead of the Douay. The Douay
is also reverent, accurate, and beautiful, but well-read
Catholics know the KJV as well as the Douay, while
well-read Protestants do not know the Douay as well as
the KJV. There are no significant theological differences
between the Catholic and the Protestant translations, at
least in the Psalms.

I have no problem with the Elizabethan, Shakespear-
ean language, with its *thee's* and *thou's*, and you should
not, either. Its meaning is not obscure, and its effect is
to announce that this is not ordinary stuff but something
extraordinary, something different, something sacred,
something holy. If the Word of God is not holy, what is?
The very word "holy" means "set apart". And if language
cannot reflect that sacredness, what can?

In another age, the danger of this emphasis on holiness,
or "set-apart-ness", might be that it is too "respectful",
too fearful, keeping God at a distance, like non-Sufi Muslims. In our age, the danger is very clearly the opposite:
an egalitarian, anti-hierarchical, anti-authoritarian flatten-
ing, a chumminess, a quotidian ordinariness, and consequent boredom. The sacred language is an *announcement*. It
sounds like trumpets. That is not a bad thing. It gets your
attention—an increasingly difficult thing to do in an age
when our souls have melted into our smartphones.

Our first prayer should be "Teach us to pray." I do not find it easy to pray, as some people do; and I have tried many things, but I keep coming back to the Psalms more and more, as I get older and (hopefully) wiser, because they "work". It is not so much a matter of *a priori* principle but a matter of *a posteriori* experience. All alternatives (except for the Lord's Prayer, the Mass, and the Rosary), however precious, fall back into secondary status for me compared with the Psalms. For these wells of wisdom open up more and more the more I pray them. They are literally inexhaustible. I guarantee you will find them so more and more if you give them a chance to sink into your subconscious by repetition.

I am only a philosopher, alas, and not a saint, a poet, or a singer. Therefore, these reflections, though they are *about* the Psalms, which are prayers, poems, and songs, are not prayers or poems or songs but only the thoughts of a philosopher, not of a saint, a poet, or a singer, like David, who was all three.

But God has graciously enabled us to make our thoughts one with our prayers. On the one hand, prayer becomes more profound by allying itself with its chief ally, thought. On the other hand, nothing makes thought more profound than becoming one with prayer.

Prayer is not easy. It is a battle. Like life. Forces of gravity—the world, the flesh, and the devil—drag us down when we seriously try to rise. Here is a weapon God Himself has inspired and given us for our great task of spiritual warfare, which is human life on earth.

Granted, the weapon does not look at first like a perfect one. Many of the psalms look at first embarrassingly primitive, selfish or self-righteous, angry, or even childish. But these very human imperfections are part of God's deliberate strategy. He could have erased them. He could have used a much more sophisticated poet and philosopher like Plato. (He did that later with Augustine.) But God works in unexpected ways. He did not use an emperor, a warrior, or a philosopher to save the world but a carpenter crucified as a criminal.

The key that He fashioned to open the locked door between Himself and you—divine revelation, the Christian religion—is a very strangely shaped key. That is because the lock in the door is a very strangely shaped lock. But the match between the key and lock is exactly right. For the divine locksmith knows both shapes as perfectly as He knows everything else.

🐝

Every good book about the Psalms mentions the following distinctive feature of Hebrew poetry: that it does not depend on the sound of its language (and therefore it translates well from one language to another) but on parallelism or repetition. A thought is stated first in one set of words, then another. The effect is like a hammer. Two nails fasten a board far better than one. This was clearly part of God's providential strategy.

Another aspect of the strategy of parallelism is to appeal to both the head and the heart, both understanding and love.

The appeal to the understanding works this way. "Say the same thought in different words" is similar to the teacher's favorite method to test whether the student understands a book or a passage: "Say it in your own words." If the student has received only the words, and not the point, he will not be able to do that. If he has understood the point, he will. Two different sets of words make the common point rise from the two sets of words as a common form rising from two pieces of matter. It abstracts from the matter (the words) to the form, the essence.

Usually, the second line (the repetition) is not quite synonymous with the first but adds a somewhat different aspect of meaning. But it is only accidentally different. The effect of this is to appeal to the reader's abstraction not of exactly the same form from different matter, like two xeroxed copies of the same page, but of the same essential form from different accidental forms, thus ensuring that the reader receives the essence, not just the accidents.

And the appeal to the heart works this way: the repetition adds nothing to the understanding of the essential point, but it adds to its force, its seriousness. The same essence is given a second existence.

❧

There are many other, better books about the Psalms than this one. Saint Augustine's sermons on the Psalms are masterpieces. C. S. Lewis, Thomas Merton, and many other religious writers have written very helpful books on the Psalms. Mine does not try to rival them, compete with them, correct them, or complete them.

Psalm 1

"Blessed is the man"

Of all the psalms we shall study, this is the shortest. Yet we will say more about this psalm than about any other. That is because this is the foundation and premise for all the other ones and the "big picture" that surrounds all the other ones. It is the key to the Psalter, the key to the front door of the spiritual house in which the Jew and the Christian and the Muslim live.

All the psalms are prayers, but this one is also an announcement, news, a truth. What kind of prayer is that? The answer is that it is a confession—not of sin, but of truth, as known by faith. Faith means, first of all, simply believing and accepting the truth that God reveals to us.

Its point is extremely simple: that life is a drama, a choice, a story, because there are two opposite ways to live and move and have our being, two opposite roads through life. They have very clear and simple names: good and evil, right and wrong, holiness and unholiness, sanctity and sin, godliness and ungodliness. And they lead inevitably to two opposite destinations: joy and misery, both in this life and after death.

> Blessed is the man that walketh not in the counsel of
>   the ungodly,
> nor standeth in the way of sinners,
> nor sitteth in the seat of the scornful.

Most parallelism doubles the initial point; this one, the first of over a thousand in the Psalms, triples it. It speaks of the same blessedness in all three of the aspects of life that are here symbolized by bodily postures: walking, standing, and sitting. "Walking" can be interpreted as one's activity, "standing" as one's identity, and "sitting" as one's enjoyments. In all three dimensions of life, blessing never comes from sin but only from sanctity.

The sins here are concretized by sinners: the "ungodly", the "sinners", and the "scornful". We must clearly distinguish sins from sinners, for we are commanded to hate sins and not sinners, and to love sinners (our "neighbors", all of whom are sinners like ourselves) and not to love sins. But we are impressed more by concretizations than abstractions; that is why examples impress us more than principles, why saints are more powerful teachers than scholars, why stories impress us more than sermons, and why great teachers always use parables. The danger is that we become so fixated on the concrete example (the person) that we take the attitude toward him that is appropriate to the principle—that is, we hate the sinner because we confuse him with the sin. This is a mistake that is natural and common to children and primitives, and it is correctable by a later sophistication and maturity of mind, when the mind becomes abstract enough to distinguish the sinner from the sin.

The opposite mistake is much harder to correct. That is the mistake of failing to begin here, with passionate and concretely real hatred of sin, as embodied in sinners. It is much easier to correct an intellectual mistake (confusing the abstract with the concrete) than to correct a mistake of the heart, and it is a mistake of the heart not to love or hate anything passionately but to be bland and indifferent, "lukewarm" (see Rev 3:16). It is much harder to warm a cold heart than to cool an overheated one, as it is much

harder to light a fire once it has gone out than to change
the direction of the air heated by the fire by adjusting the
air vents. It is harder to make a saint out of an ice cube than
out of a firebrand, just as it is harder to start up a car that is
stuck than to change its direction once it is moving. David
speaks like a primitive or a child, but like a primitive saint,
a saintly child. We speak like sophisticated scholars, but we
are lukewarm. We need contact with primitives like David
more than we need contact with scholars like ourselves.

❦

This first verse is an *announcement*, a truth-claim, a prophecy. It is controversial. It is not a platitude. In fact, it is so
far from a platitude that it does not *seem* to be true at all.
Let us be totally honest: we religious believers, who try,
however feebly, to walk God's straight road instead of sin's
crooked roads, do not *seem* to be especially blessed. The
meek do not seem to inherit the earth. Job does not seem
to be blessed, sitting there on his dung heap, having lost
his children, his possessions, and the respect of his wife
and his friends. Martyrs do not seem to be blessed when
they are crucified, drawn and quartered, beheaded, hanged,
tortured, fed to lions, boiled in oil, etc. When we read the
lives of the saints, we do not envy or seriously emulate
their deliberately chosen mortifications and sacrifices and
ascetical practices.

There is another reason why our religion seems at first
to be far from a blessing: because it imposes limitations
and obligations on us. It seems to be full of "nos" and
"nots", such as the three mentioned in this verse. He that
"sitteth in the seat of the scornful" says that our "nots"
tie us in knots, while he is free for his sinning and scorn-
ing. We seem to have fewer options and more limitations

than carefree, freewheeling secularists. We pray "Thy will
be done", while they say "My will be done." We sing
"God's way is the best way", while they sing "I did it my
way." And while God's will is one, my will is many. It is
full of attractive "diversity". It is a broad road, with many
options. God's is a straight and narrow one.

The Koran begins with the same road map as the Psalms:

"In the name of Allah ("The One God"), the Most Gracious, the Most Merciful: All praise is due to Allah, Lord
of the Universe, the Most Gracious, the Most Merciful,
Owner of the Day of Judgment. You alone do we worship, to You alone we turn for help. Guide us to the straight
path, the path of those on whom You have bestowed Your
grace, not the way of those who have earned Your anger,
of those who have gone astray."

That is what this psalm is about: the two ways. There
are only two. As C. S. Lewis puts it, in *The Great Divorce*,
"there are only two kinds of people, in the end: those
who say to God, 'Thy will be done,' and those to whom
God says, in the end, '*Thy* will be done.'"

So this verse should startle us. It is *news*. It tells us that
we who choose to walk the straight path, however wob-
blingly, are the real winners and that the sinners and scorn-
ers who call us "losers" are the real losers.

And not just in the next life, as if that were God's com-
pensation to us for our losses in this life. David is speaking
of both this life, in verses 1, 2, and 4, whose verbs are all
in the present tense, and the next life, in verses 3, 5, and 6,
whose verbs are all in the future tense and can be interpreted as referring to the future either in this life or in the
next, or, most likely, both.

We are all sinners, of course. But "the scornful" do not
admit it or do anything about it, and they scorn and pity
and sneer at those of us who do. The damned do not go

to Hell because they sin but because they scorn and sneer at the idea of sin and repentance. They are scornful to those of us who hate the sins that they love. The difference between the damned and the blessed is not that one class sins and the other does not, but that one class scorns and the other repents, that the one class is happy with their sins and the other is unhappy with them.

❧

But "unhappy" does not *look* like "blessed".

Looks can be deceiving. To be happy with saints and with sanctity is to be blessed, but to be happy with sinners and with sins is not to be blessed. We are not blessed for hating sinners, but we are blessed for hating sins, not for sinning, and we are blessed even less for being happy with our sins. "Nonjudgmental" people who hate nothing, not even sin, think they are saints because they hate nothing, because they do not judge. But because they do not judge and discriminate, they are really eating poison along with food. For sin is to the soul what poison is to the body. True, we are told to "judge not [i.e., do not judge *sinners*], that ye be not judged." But those who do not judge *sins will* be judged.

They think they are blessed because they feel happy with their sins. They are wrong. Feeling happy is not the same as really being happy; or, more clearly put, real blessedness is not merely felt happiness or contentment with just anything we please. Drugs do not bless even when they deliver a "high". Sin is a drug and an addiction. We are sinaholics.

We live in a culture that tolerates anything except intolerance. Our culture judges anyone who does not follow this broad and tolerant and nonjudgmental road as *not* blessed. They are wrong. Saints are blessed, even when they sit on Job's dung heap, and sinners are not blessed even when they sit on a mountain of gold. That is the startling news that Jesus teaches in the Beatitudes.

This psalm is startling in the same way Jesus is. It sees behind appearances and the present and into reality and the future. It says, implicitly, that "All things work together for good [for blessing] to them that love God" (Rom 8:28). It says that even things that seem or feel *not* good or blessed, like sacrifices and sufferings, work together for good. And even things that are not good at all, like tragedies, eventually work together for the greater good; if not, God would not allow them. And even sins can work together for good, but only through sincere repentance. This startling verse also implies that all things work together for misery and failure for those who do not love God and what God is (*agape*, unselfish love: cf. 1 Jn 4:8), even the things that seem good and blessed, like worldly success and contentment.

What this psalm says, then, is startling and hard to believe. If you do not spontaneously find it startling, you do not understand it. It is not just that sinners have more red ink (losses) than black (gains, profit) in the final accounting, while saints have more black than red. It is that *everything* is black ink for the one who loves righteousness and everything is red ink for the one who loves sin.

By the way, David does not focus on any specialized sins or virtues here. If you are thinking only of sins of the flesh here, such as lust and greed and hedonism, think again. If you are thinking only of the cold, calculating sins of the spirit here, such as pride and self-righteousness, think again. The sins you think about the least may well be the ones that are harming you the most.

As we stated before, all of life is included in the three symbolic postures of this verse: walking (our actions), standing (our identity), and sitting (our rest, enjoyment, and contemplation, our spiritual home). Watchman Nee, the Chinese Protestant mystic, wrote a fine little book, entitled *Sit, Walk, Stand*, about how Saint Paul uses these three postures in Ephesians. Check it out.

The truth of the all-or-nothing claim of this psalm, its picture of life as divided into these two and only these two roads, is not seen with the eyes or with the mind-without-faith. It is believed. It is not *apparently* true. Faith often contradicts appearances. That is why it is controversial and easy to scorn. It is not innate or automatic. It is not natural. It is supernatural. It takes effort and choice. But whether it is true or false, it is certainly not an obvious cliché or a boring platitude. The claims of biblical religion are either an amazing truth or a ridiculous insanity.

That does not mean that faith is irrational. "I believe it because God said it" is not irrational. "God may have said it, but I don't want to believe it"—that is irrational.

Faith is also testable in life. Ask any saint.

🐝

The most fundamental and universal claim of all the religions in the world is that there is an absolute objective reality that transcends us, that is our *summum bonum*, or greatest good, our final end and purpose and "meaning of life", and that explains and orders everything in our lives. For Jews, Christians, and Muslims, this is the God of Abraham, the personal Creator of the universe. But all religions (and even all unbelievers, through conscience) know some slice, however thin, of this God, some Absolute Good. The slice believers know also is very, very thin compared to what God really is. Our only claim is that the slice God has revealed through these Scriptures is significantly thicker than any other.

This truth-claim, this religious or theological or meta-physical or objective or theoretical point, logically entails a second one, which is the human, moral, practical, or psychological point, namely, that although there is only one Absolute Reality, there are for us two roads that we must choose between. The first road comes from and leads to this Absolute Reality. The second road does not.

A third point follows: that the good road is one, since God, the Real Absolute, is one, while the evil road is manifold, since there are manifold idols or false absolutes. As Chesterton sagely said, there is only one angle at which one can stand upright but a thousand angles at which one can fall. As Aristotle said, for every virtue there are two opposite vices, since every virtue puts right order into our actions and passions, so that there can be two kinds of disorder: too much and too little of any action or passion. For instance, recklessness and cowardice are the two alternatives to courage; shamefaced shyness and shamelessness are the two alternatives to modesty; insensitivity and self-indulgence are the two alternatives to moderation in the appetites, etc.

These three points, this threefold affirmation, is not a theory; it is a fact. It is testable and provable by experience, by experiments in the laboratory of life. It is a kind of spiritual geography, and it is as factual as physical geography. There are, in fact, two opposite roads, up and down. And no amount of sincerity or honest mistakes can turn one road into the other. Evil does not become good by our believing and willing it. Good does not become evil by our refusing it. Spiritual roads lead to different destinations just as surely as physical roads do. You cannot get to the Pacific Ocean by walking east from Philadelphia, no matter how sincere you are. And you cannot get to God or Heaven by faithlessness, hopelessness, or lovelessness no matter how hard or how sincerely you try. Morals are as objective as mathematics, and metaphysics is as ojective as physics, though known by different instruments.

The "only two objectively real roads" claim does not apply to material goods. What is personally and practically and materially good for one person may not be good for another in matters of food, entertainment, mates, careers, or numbers of children. But in moral matters, that relativity does not hold. Morality is obligatory for all, since all are human, all are equal in having human nature. If that is not so, we are open to racism, sexism, and even genocide, some being "less human" than others. We are differently handicapped (all of us are handicapped in some way; only God is not), but we are not differently human, and therefore we are not differently obligated morally. No one may hate, murder, steal, rape, cheat, lie, enslave, or disrespect. All are called to altruism, justice, honesty, courage, kindness, humility, and respect. The two roads are objective and universal, and our obligation to choose the road of good rather than evil is absolute.

The ancient Chinese concept of yin and yang says that at the heart of each thing we find its opposite: pain and pleasure, life and death, light and darkness, success and failure. They are relative to each other, dependent on each other. This may be true for all material goods but not for moral goods. Moral goodness does not have at its heart moral evil, nor is moral evil really good at heart. Even though we are mixtures of saints and sinners, sanctity is not sin, and sin is not sanctity. Even though there is a little good in the worst of us and a little bad in the best of us, yet there is not a little good in badness or a little bad in goodness.

Even though, as Solzhenitsyn famously said, the division between good and evil does not run between nations, cultures, races, or ideologies but through the middle of every human heart, the division itself is absolute. We may have one foot on one road and one foot on the other; we may prefer a blend and a compromise; but the roads themselves fork, they do not blend.

What the religion of the Bible joins to this universally known absolute morality is an absolute theology that is *not* universally known. The gods of other religions are either many (and thus no one of them is the supreme good) or else half-good and half-evil, or beyond good and evil. The God of Judaism, which is the God Christians and Muslims have learned to believe in, is "light, and in him is no darkness at all" (1 Jn 1:5).

❦

The psalm uses three terms for three degrees of those who choose the evil road: first, "the ungodly", then "sinners", then "the scornful". There is a progression here. "The ungodly" refers to a lack of godliness, a sin of omission; "sinners" refers to positive acts of sin, and "the scornful" refers to the darkest depth of the most Satanic sin, sneering pride. George MacDonald says that a sneer does more harm to the soul than a murder.

As there are these three dimensions of evil, there are also three dimensions of life, symbolized by the three life-postures of sitting, walking, and standing that we have already discussed. The evil are "walking" (living) according to the counsel (practical philosophy) of the ungodly, are "standing" in the way of sinners, i.e., waiting for some temptation to sin to come their way rather than running from it and toward God, and "sitting" in the comfortable seat of the scornful, looking down their noses at the righteous.

The ungodly are "walking" away from God. No one can be neutral or static in relation to God; every change is either toward Him and Heaven or away from Him and toward Hell. They are also "standing" in the wrong place, identifying with the wrong friends and the wrong things. Worst of all, the scornful sneerer is "sitting" comfortably in the catbird seat and looking down his turned-up nose at those silly, simple-minded sissies who are sincerely struggling against sin.

❦

The Psalmist shows us that the way of the righteous necessarily has two dimensions: negative and positive, what the righteous man does not do (v. 1) and what he does do (v. 2). One cannot have either of these two aspects without the other. There are only two roads, therefore "Don't take road A" and "Do take road B" logically entail each other. A merely negative morality (a list of "don't's" or sins) and a merely positive morality (a list of "do's" or ideals) are both radically incomplete. "Do good" and "avoid evil" are two sides of the same coin, two dimensions of the same way of life. "Do evil" and "avoid good" are two sides of the opposite coin, the opposite way.

There are not many ways, only two. There is good, and there is evil. There is light, and there is darkness. There is right, and there is wrong. There is sanctity, and there is sin. One cannot embrace sanctity without rejecting sin, and one cannot embrace sin without rejecting sanctity. For "no man can serve two masters" (Mt 6:24). There is no third option, and there is no pacifism possible, because we are in the middle of a battlefield. In every act, we are either doing God's work and fighting the devil or doing the devil's work and fighting God. "Spiritual warfare" is not an abstract ideology, it is a concrete fact. When we finally are honest enough to face that fact, when we wake up from our comfortable dream and see that those things that look like butterflies are really bullets and those things that look like rocks are really land mines, we will find that a new consciousness will click in, a wartime consciousness. (This happened to us when we first saw those images of 9/11 on TV. Remember?) Adrenaline will flow, and we will regain our clear focus and get our priorities straight. No one complains about lumpy beds or stale bread on a battlefield.

That does not mean that we are either simply saints or simply sinners. We are both, and the saints are very clear about that. Saints always know they are sinners, while sinners often think they are saints. Both sides shuttle back and forth across the battlefield, occasionally making compromises with their enemy, whether their enemy is God or the devil. But our hearts, though often fickle and unfaithful, are married to one or the other. "No man can serve two masters" because there *are* only two masters to serve: the true God or the false god, God or self.

These two roads are not abstractions, "goodness" and "badness". They are concrete roads that really exist and that take us to concrete destinations, to real places, though not in this universe, to two real eternal destinations. Both of them are utterly unimaginable, yet utterly real. Heaven does not really have harps and golden streets—it is much, much better than that; and Hell does not really have pitchforks and physical fire—it is much, much worse than that.

> But his delight is in the law of the LORD;
> and in his law doth he meditate day and night.

The Psalmist now makes a second controversial, prophetic, and surprising affirmation: that this "straight and narrow road" and this "moralistic" God, who issues *Commandments* (and in no other religion does God issue absolute Commandments!), lead, not to repression and depression, but to *delight*. And the delight is not in spite of God's Law but because of it. It is delight "in" the Law.

This is not easy to understand, because the Law is not some beautiful ideal, like a mountaintop, or a set of personal "values" that we can buy into if and when we want to. The Law is not "suggestions" or "ideals" or "values". God did not give Moses ten "values". "Values" sounds safely abstract, like a cloud or like the Pillsbury Dough Boy; but "law" is hard and sharp, like a sword. It is uncomfortably clear and definite. "Values" are vague and hard to understand but easy to live; God's Commandments are clear and easy to understand but hard to live.

The Law is perfect, but we are not. We are incapable of keeping God's Law perfectly. The Law of God is our unflattering X ray that shows us up for what we are: stupid, selfish, shallow sinners. Although the Law is full of light and wisdom and perfection, it cannot save us because we cannot obey it. It is not the good news of our healing operation but the bad news of our revealing X ray.

Why, then, would a pious Old Testament Jew delight in contemplating the X ray that showed him his deadly heart disease?

The answer is certainly not that the Jews were self-righteous like the Pharisees, who thought they were obedient to the Law and good enough to deserve Heaven. Jews, like Christians and Muslims, are big on justice, because God is; but (again like Christians and Muslims) when they pray to God, they do not ask for justice but for mercy. The most perfect saints, both then and now, both Jewish and Christian (and Muslim), were those who knew how imperfect they were by the infallible and non-negotiable standards of God's perfect Law. Many Christians used to be taught that Judaism was a religion of law and fear and condemnation while Christianity was a religion of love and trust and hope. It was not just an oversimplification or an exaggeration; it was a lie.

What is not at first clear is *why* the Law caused delight to the pious Old Testament Jew; but what is clear is that the pious Jew did in fact delight in the Law. Why else would one choose to meditate on anything day and night unless it caused delight? One meditates on the face of his beloved, or on a great work of art that he is creating, or on the feast he is about to share with his best friends. One does not meditate on the Internal Revenue Service's tax code or on the traffic regulations of his police department. So the Psalmist must see God's Law as something more like the face of his beloved than something like the laws of the state regulating the movement of money or vehicles. How can we understand this?

Only if we understand God, who is pure joy and delight *because He is love*, and love is the greatest joy and delight. That is what is behind all the threats and disciplines and punishments: the love of a Heavenly Father, who is not only hard to satisfy but also easy to please. "The fear of the LORD is the beginning of wisdom" (Prov 9:10) indeed, but it is not the end. Love is the end. God's Law is for nothing less than love and from nothing less than love. That is why it sparks delight. Love—not the nice feeling but the fact, the deed, the choice, the will to the good of the other—is "the fulfillment of the Law". The summary of the Jewish Law—the whole Law, "the Law and the Prophets", i.e., all of divine revelation—is the two great commandments to love the Lord your God with your

whole heart and soul and mind and strength and to love
your neighbor as yourself.

The key is not in the word "law" but in the word
"Lord". The object of the Psalmist's delight is not law as
such, but "the law of the LORD". His Law is His will, the
will of our Lover and our Beloved. And His will toward
us is motivated by one thing (God is wonderfully single-
minded): love, His love of us, of our true good, and of
our true delight. The Law is really His spiritual face, and
He is the Psalmist's beloved, so the Law is, indeed, to the
Psalmist the face of his beloved!

To the pious Jew of Old Testament times, the Law was
our umbilical cord to God, our bridge from God to us and
from us to God. The Law was to him in a similar position
to the position that Christ is to Christians: the bridge, the
glue, the road that connects us to God. The Law was God's
Word and God's will. Through it he could know God and
His perfect, beautiful righteousness. (The most beautiful
thing in the world is a saint!) This affirmation, once made,
is life-changing.

The pagans did not know this. Their gods were not righteous; they were as wicked as we are. For they were made
in our own image. But the God of the Jews was certainly
not made in man's image, for He was all light, with no
"dark side", unlike either the many gods of paganism or the
one God of pantheism. Once we know this, we are turned
right side up. We stop making God in our own image.

The Fall turned us all upside down, so that our faces are
turned to the ground and our noses to the grindstone and
our feet are kicking up in rebellion at the sky. God turns us
right side up, so that when we look at Him now, we look
up, at perfect goodness, perfect light and life and love. And
this gives us a whole new philosophy of life utterly different from pagan polytheism. It gives us the true road to the

joy we all seek: the practice of the goodness, righteousness, and holiness that God is.

For all men seek delight, but not all seek moral rectitude. The main reason we do not love the road of moral rectitude is that it seems to lack delight, and the main reason we are tempted to the other road is that it promises delight. If Adam's apple had looked rotten or wormy, it would not have served Satan's purposes. If sin did not look like fun, we would all be saints. The devil is a deceiver. He baits his ugly, rusty hook with fat, juicy worms. If we saw through his lie and believed God's truth, if we believed the opposite of what we habitually believe, if we believed that only the straight and narrow road is delightful and not the broad road that leads to destruction—in other words, if we believed Psalm 1—then our innate love of delight would be glued to a love of the divine Law, and the energy that motivates our running down the road to sin—the energy that is our love of joy—would motivate our running up the road to sanctity.

And that is exactly what the Psalmist claims here for the life of faith. The more we believe what this Psalm asserts, the more holy and therefore the more happy we will be. That faith is the beginning of everything and the heart of the ongoing struggle. We must constantly pray to the Lord, "Increase our faith" (Lk 17:5) and "Lord, I believe; help thou mine unbelief" (Mk 9:24).

But faith is testable. This startling claim is testable. "Try it, you'll like it."

How can we meditate "day and night" if we are not monks in monasteries? When we read these words, we see an image in our minds of a man (why never a woman?) in a robe reading a prayer book. If he is not a monk, he is at least an ancient Jew or Greek or Roman in premodern times when they had time to do things like meditate: no phones, cars, radios, TVs, computers, or email.

Modern thechnology changes very little, really. Mankind cannot change its essence, only its accidents. Therefore, this verse applies to us harried, hassled moderns just as much as it applies to any premodern (whose harries and hassles were different from ours but probably just as problematic).

Yet it is also true that we have significantly different harries and hassles because of the invention of the clock, and thus of a different kind of time (kronos, or chronos, time measured scientifically and quantitatively by matter's movements through space rather than kairos, time measured personally and qualitatively by purpose and design). So how can we moderns possibly meditate "day and night"? That does not "fit into our schedule".

We can do this today in at least three short and simple ways. They will all make a different kind of a difference and produce a result way out of proportion to the effort we put into them.

First, at least two special sacred times should be set aside for conscious, deliberate prayer and meditation every day and every night. Start short. If we are too ambitious in this, we will simply give it up. So I suggest that if we do not yet do it at all, we begin by making it a very short time: perhaps five minutes during the day and five minutes at night before we retire, when we are tired and not fit for long meditations. Actually doing, faithfully, a little thing that is doable is much better than dreaming of doing, but not doing, a much greater thing. A mouse is greater than a dragon because it actually exists.

Second, the Morning Offering should be the first words from our lips when we arise, and though that takes only a minute or two (perhaps another minute to place ourselves first in the presence of God and then a minute or two or three to say the prayer), it "counts" for the whole day, makes a difference to the whole day, just as much as the fact that you are male or female, white or black, old or young makes a difference to everything you do during the day. You have given God your whole day; do you think He does not hear you, notice you, care about this, accept it, or take you at your word? Does He have A.D.D. like you?

Third, it is fairly easy to develop the habit of frequent short prayer "bursts" during the day. Three of the many forms they can take are:

(1) "thank-you's" for the good stuff (and once you begin to "count your blessings", you will be amazed at their multitude);

(2) "help-me's" for the bad stuff (and remember that *no* prayer is ever unanswered, and when they are not answered in your way they are answered in God's way, and God's way is always better and wiser than your way); and

(3) "OK's" or "Thy will be done's" or just silent nods or salutes for choices to obey what your conscience tells you is His will for you—and when this involves sacrifice, the pain of these sacrifices will always turn into joy sooner or later.

And please do not take these suggestions as *alternatives* to longer, more intense prayer times.

And he shall be like a tree planted by the rivers of water,
that bringeth forth his fruit in his season;
his leaf also shall not wither;
and whatsoever he doeth shall prosper.

In the Bible, trees typically symbolize life. The "Tree of Life" in the Garden of Eden was not just an ordinary literal, physical tree like all others, with merely vegetative life. It was, or symbolized, something far higher than that. Genesis says that God planted it: it was a God-tree. It symbolized the very life of God in the soul, divine life, eternal life, supernatural life, Heavenly life, spiritual life, sanctifying grace, *zoe*. Our plug-in to God's life makes our soul lovely, large, and leafy, like a tree. We are to rise and expand. Today, the Psalmist might use the image of electricity to make the point. We are to become lively, a "live wire". We have more *energy* when we see God's wise and beautiful plan for our lives, which culminates in nothing less than sainthood, superabundant goodness, an obedience to His Law that is not dour and servile but that jumps for joy, because that obedience is out of love; it is nothing less than love-in-action; and nothing is more beautiful than love-in-action because that is what God is, what God is made of through and through.

Every living thing needs water, but this thing, this tree, is planted by *rivers* of water, not just little brooks. This water is not a trickle, but like an ocean, and we surf on its waves, the waves of divine grace, divine love. It cannot be bottled and contained for our consumption. It is much bigger, not smaller, than we are. It is a mighty roaring, rushing river. Nothing can contain it. It is unimpeded, uncontrollable, and undying. And it is not comfortably lukewarm; it is bracing and cold and startlingly refreshing.

This water is also fire. It is the fire of God's own life with which He wants to kindle our souls. To change the image one more time, He wants to infect our souls with a good infection, with a healing of the disease that is our other infection; with a "possession" that is the opposite of demonic possession, for we are truly His possessions, not the devil's. He wants to haunt us with His Holy Ghost, who is infinitely more formidable than any other ghost (spirit).

We are *planted* by this water; we are not just *visiting* the water like a tourist. We are rooted and planted there to stay. Our whole identity is there. We are totally committed to this new home, by this new river, so that if we are uprooted from it, we die and simply have no identity left at all. (For true religion is a life-or-death thing, an everything-or-nothing thing.)

When we are planted by this river, we bring forth fruit. A tree is known by its fruit as a cause is known by its effects. You cannot have the effect without the cause. We cannot bring forth the fruits of faith without faith. We cannot attain either personal peace or social justice, both of which are fruits of this tree, without that water, which infinitely transcends both personal peace and social justice. To worship the fruits of the life instead of the One who is the Source of the life is idolatry. Two common forms of idolatry today, especially among Christians, are the worship of personal peace or happiness or contentment or any other psychological state or feeling and the worship of social justice. (Only very good and important things can function as idols; nobody worships Draino or post-it notes.)

The fruit of this tree is organic, not mechanical; it is "brought forth" from within the tree, not added to it from without. And therefore it must grow gradually, "in its season", rather than according to the seasons of our will, which in a technological age demands instant gratification, as if the tree were a machine with buttons to push. Its growth requires patience as well as impatience, like Job or like a pregnant woman.

Although it grows, like material plants, it does not decay and wither and die like them, for this is a spiritual plant. Its "leaf", its fruit, "does not wither" but lasts forever. What lasts forever? Only the life of God, which we are, incredibly, designed to share by His grace. That is why whatever the man who is planted by this water does shall "prosper". Nothing that is done by the wicked will prosper. The wicked are conquered by time, oppressed by time, obsessed with time, harried and hassled by time. The righteous are conquerors of time. Time is their servant, not their master.

It sometimes seems as if this picture of the two lives is not true; for we often seem to see the righteous failing to prosper, being poor and taken advantage of, and even martyred. And it seems that we see the wicked prospering, making billions, and controlling the corridors of power in the world's capitals. Or else it seems that both the saints and the sinners prosper randomly, at some times and in some things and not others. Yet the psalm contradicts this: it says that *whatever* the righteous "tree-man" does will prosper and, in the next verse, that *nothing* that the wicked does will prosper.

How do we solve this problem? How can the Psalmist say such things that seem to contradict what appears to our senses? Obviously, one or both of the following two distinctions are implied here: between appearance and the reality that is really going on behind the appearances; and between the present world-system, where injustice appears sometimes to be more profitable than justice, and the world to come that is to last forever, in which justice always profits and wickedness never does.

The more important of the two distinctions is the first one; for even now, as Plato clearly saw, "justice is more profitable than injustice" (that is the final conclusion of his *Republic*), and "it is better [not just more moral but also more profitable, more happifying] to suffer evil than to do it." Even now, there is empirical, sensory, physical

evidence that Plato was right. You can see saints and martyrs die with smiles on their faces and hymns on their lips,
forgiving their murderers; and you can also see the angry,
unhappy, strained muscles in the faces of the wicked, the
hot, unhappy hate in their eyes, and the shrillness in their
voices. And when they suppress the rage without, you can
still sense the rage within. This is a foretaste of Heaven and
Hell. Let those who have eyes to see, see.

Not just some things, or even many things, but every
single thing in the lives of the righteous "shall prosper".
"*All* things work together for good to them that love God"
(Rom 8:28). This is true even now in fact though not always
in appearances; and it will become apparent in the future,
partly in this world and totally in the next. The reason why
this must be so is that nothing but God, nothing but what
God is, what God is "made of", nothing but truth, goodness, and beauty, and ultimately nothing but love can satisfy
our souls. For nothing else can have such a total and universal effect, like light, which illumines not some but all colors
and shapes. Everything else is partial: health, money, power,
success, pleasures, stuff. Matter has parts outside of parts.
One chunk of stuff cannot coexist with another. Matter is
competitive. Matter is proud of itself and its "territory". But
that is not true of spiritual things, of soul-stuff, of truth or
goodness or beauty. Spirit is not proud but humble. It gives
itself away.

This divine life is like light. That is why it is universal, not partial. No color or shape is universal, only light
is. When it shines, all colors and shapes are fulfilled. The
more light, the more redness and the more blueness and
the more yellowness. And in darkness, there are no colors at all. The difference is not between this and that but
between everything and nothing. Religion (which means
"relationship" with God) is "all or nothing". For either

God is everything, as the saints say, or nothing, as the atheists say. Either everything the saints do "prospers" because
they stand planted by a river that is the life of God, or
nothing they do prospers because they are fools who live
in the same waterless desert as the wicked, and they are
only imagining this divine river. In fact, the river is real,
but the wicked see only desert where the righteous see the
water. The wicked have only two eyes, but the righteous
have the third eye of faith, which has X-ray vision.

At the end of the last of C.S. Lewis' *Chronicles of Narnia*,
The Last Battle, a group of cynical and unbelieving dwarfs
are taken into the presence of Aslan (who is the Son of God
incarnate in Narnia), but they stubbornly close their eyes
(and their hearts) and refuse to open them. They chant,
"The dwarfs are for the dwarfs." They are in Hell. Some
of the saints say that Heaven and Hell are really the same
place: those who love what Heaven is made of—God's
absolute truth and absolute love and absolute beauty—will
be blissed and blessed by it, while those who hate and fear
such demanding threats to the ego and its autonomy will
be tortured by those very same divine attributes, which are
inescapable. The same light that delights the good tortures
the evil because they hate the light. As Christ said, "men
loved darkness rather than light, because their deeds were
evil" (Jn 3:19). All get what they want, in the end. "Blessed
are they which do hunger and thirst after righteousness: for
they shall be filled" (Mt 5:6). And woe to those who hunger for unrighteousness: for they also shall be filled.

> The ungodly are not so: but are like the chaff
> which the wind driveth away.

The chaff is the hard, inedible outside of the edible grain,
especially the wheat from which bread is made. After

the grain is harvested, it is winnowed: the chaff is separated from the wheat and thrown away to the wind. The
wheat shares in the beautiful and meaningful destiny of
being made into bread, being eaten and being transformed
into part of the body of human beings, while the chaff
loses even its vegetable life and becomes lifeless dust in
the wind. The wheat becomes more than itself, while the
chaff becomes less than itself. We, too, must become either
more than ourselves, sharing in the very life of God, or less
than ourselves, less than human. What lives in Hell is not
human beings but ex-human beings.

Our pictures of Hell are much too flattering to the
damned: we picture them as human beings, such as we
now know them, in a torture chamber. But they have lost
their humanity; they have lost their wheat, they have
lost their capacity to become part of the life of God; they
are only "chaff", detritus, garbage. C. S. Lewis, in *The
Great Divorce*, describes a minor character in Hell who is
only a grumbling old lady. Her sin is not spectacular, but
there is nothing but that sin in her. She is no longer "a
grumbler" but "only a grumble". She has lost her "I", her
image of God (Who is "I AM"). "What shall it profit a
man, if he shall gain the whole world, and lose his own
soul", his very self? (Mk 8:36).

We are the wheat, and our destiny is to share God's life,
to be "eaten" by God. When we consume the sacred Host
in the Eucharist, we do not digest God or transform God;
God "digests" us and transforms us. Similarly, when Christ
was baptized in the Jordan, the water did not change Him;
He changed the water and gave it the power to communicate His divine life to us in baptism.

This life is active, as both water and fire are active.
That is why Scripture uses both symbols for it. The
Book of Wisdom pictures the souls in Heaven as sparks

moving, darting, and dancing among the reeds. They are supremely active. This psalm pictures the souls in Hell as chaff, passive and unfree, driven by the wind, not by their own choices. We can understand Heaven and Hell only in images, in earthly analogies. Sparks and chaff are two of the best ones.

> Therefore the ungodly shall not stand in the judgment,
> nor sinners in the congregation of the righteous.

There are, after all, only two ways to live and two states in which to die: with a living soul or with a dead soul. (Souls can die. That is what Hell is: not eternal life with pain, but eternal death.)

The righteous are trees "planted" firmly by the living water of the river, but the wicked are "driven *away*" on the dry, dead wind. They cannot "stand" in the light of the judgment: the light kills them. They cannot stand up with the rest of the congregation of the righteous because chaff has no legs. They can neither sit (relax, enjoy) nor walk (choose, work, act, accomplish) nor stand (maintain their identity)—the three postures that symbolize the three dimensions of human life. They have lost their souls, their human souls, their humanity. For, ever since Christ joined divinity and humanity in His own person, no one can find or lose either divinity or humanity without finding or losing the other one as well.

If the wicked mingled with the righteous at the Judgment, they would be tortured by the light, so God in His mercy says "Depart from Me." For the closer they are to the divine fire, the more they burn. It is not His hate that alienates them and tortures them, but His love and mercy. He hates no one, not even the worst sinner; He hates only sins, even the smallest sins, precisely *because*

He loves sinners. We are to become more and more like
Him, hating sinners less and less (including ourselves)
and hating sins more and more (especially our own). The
more the doctor loves the patient, the more he hates
the cancer.

> For the LORD knoweth the way of the righteous:
> but the way of the ungodly shall perish.

That first little word of the last verse ("for") is important
because it clues us in to the fact that here, in what follows
that word, is the ultimate reason for everything else in the
psalm (and in life). All the rest of this psalm is true only
because of ("for") this last verse.

This requires explanation.

What is "the way of the righteous"? It is Jesus Christ. He
is "the way" as well as "the truth" and "the life" (Jn 14:6)

In this psalm, we find Christ. In this psalm, we find not
just the Law but the Gospel, the Good News. Here comes
Christ charging into David's psalm, in the last verse. Or
rather, not "here He comes" (from outside), but "here
He is, within, all the time, in disguise." He is everywhere
in the Old Testament. Not by name, but by substance.
Every word in Scripture is a cell in His face, His portrait.
Every word in "the Word of God" that is the Bible is part
of the Word of God that is Christ. He is the unity of the
Bible. That is why Augustine says, in his *Confessions*, that
the second time he read the Bible it was totally different
from the first time, when he had despised it as lacking
in classical beauty and sophisticated wisdom compared to
Cicero: because the second time, after his conversion, he
saw it aright, for in it "I saw One Face." He saw the Word
in the word. We should see the same. But it will take a
little time to see it. Please be patient.

To see how this psalm is about Christ, we need to begin at the beginning.

The obvious point of this whole psalm is that there are only two roads, two ways of life, and therefore only two kinds of people: the righteous, or the godly, who are blessed, and the wicked, or the ungodly, who are "not so". It does not follow that we can know who is in each class. We know *what* but not *who*. That is something only God knows, since only God sees into the heart of the heart. Appearances can be deceiving. The line between good people and evil people is muddy, though the line between good and evil is clear.

Back to that word "for". *Why* are the righteous blessed and the wicked not? The last verse tells us: because God "knows" the "way" of the righteous but not the way of the wicked. For the godly are Godlike, and God knows Himself. Therefore, the way of the righteous, like God, lasts forever, and so will they, while the way of the wicked will perish, and so will they. But what does this mean?

Only the New Testament makes it fully clear. "The way of the righteous" is not a set of abstract laws or principles or ideas, but it is Jesus Christ Himself, who says "*I am* the way." He is not merely the teacher of the way, like all great prophets and philosophers, saints and sages; He IS the way. Our way of life is not a road map, but a road. Better, it is a vehicle. Better yet, it is a driver. The Word of God is, first of all, not on paper but on wood: the wood of the Cross.

He says that He is (1) "the way", and (2) "the truth", and (3) "the life" (Jn 14:6). What does this mean?

(1) Let us begin with "the way". Christ is what Lao Tzu's *Tao Te Ching* calls "the way" (*Tao*). This means to Lao Tzu three things. It means (a) the way of ultimate reality, the way reality is and works: by unselfish

love, by self-giving. (2) This is manifested in all of nature, as the mind of the artist is manifested in the matter of his art. How is it manifested? In things like water, which gives itself away to all living things. In fact, everything gives something of itself to other beings: gravity, electrical energy, heat, life, food, procreation, work, art. (3) It is also the way of life of the wise man who lives in this reality, and lives it out. Hieromonk Damascene persuasively argues, in *Christ the Eternal Tao*, that the author of this poem knew Christ more profoundly than any other pagan thinker in history.

(2) He is also the "truth", the Logos, the Mind of God, God's self-revelation, the ultimate truth, the most important thing knowable, the nature of ultimate reality, the goal sought by all the great philosophers and always only partially found.

(3) And He is the Life, the thing Nietzsche sadly found lacking in Christianity: the fire, the beauty, the power, the Lion. He is *zoe*, supernatural life, the very life of God incarnated in human flesh.

These are the three things we all want. They correspond to the three attributes of Brahman, the supreme God, in Hinduism: *sat-chit-ananda*. *Sat* is eternal life, *chit* is eternal truth, and *ananda* is eternal bliss and joy and beauty through the way of love, our participation in this supernatural life by selfless love. These three things, "the way, the truth, and the life", correspond to the three powers of the human soul that raise us above the beasts: the will, the head, and the heart. Saint John, in his first Epistle, repeatedly calls them "life", "light", and "love", the three things God is, the three things Christ manifests.

God manifested these three divine attributes by instituting three holy offices in the Old Testament, all of which were fulfilled by Christ: kings, prophets, and priests. (They correspond to the captain, the navigator, and the sailors on a ship.) This is why all our great epics have three heroes, three protagonists: Aragorn, Gandalf, and Frodo in *The Lord of the Rings*; Captain Kirk, Mr. Spock, and "Bones" McCoy in *Star Trek*; Dmitri, Ivan, and Alyosha Karamazov in *The Brothers Karamazov*; Quint, Hooper, and Brody in *Jaws*; Peter, John, and James in the Gospels.

Now apply that to this psalm. God knows "the way of the righteous", and Christ is the "way" of the righteous. As the Son of the Father, He exists because the Father "knows" Him into being eternally, beginninglessly, and endlessly. He is the very Word or Revelation or Thought of the Father. This Word is both "with" God the Father, as another Person, and "is" God, the same single God, in one nature, one essence, one substance, one being (Jn 1:1–2). God is one "what" in three "whos".

Christ is God's "Word", and when God speaks His word—e.g., "Let there be light"—the light comes into being, because of this creative Word. Christ is "in the beginning" and so He is in the beginning of the Bible. God creates by His Word, by Christ. This Word is not a label that comes *after* the thing labeled. This Word does not come after the thing; this Word comes before the thing, this Word makes the thing—as in human art. It is like Tolkien making hobbits out of that newly coined word, "hobbit", which came first in Tolkien's mind before it came to be in his art, in his created world.

So things get their being only in God's Word. And so do we. But God's Word is a Person. It is Christ.

The principle is mind-blowing. For God, being does not precede and determine knowledge or love, as it does for us (except in creative art, as in the above example of "hobbits"). We know (discover) and love (desire) a previously existing world and the things and persons in it. But

God knows and loves the world and human persons into existence! For God, love and knowledge (His "word") determine being; being does not determine knowledge and love. He does not discover the world or fall in love with it, as we do. He creates it—its truth by His knowing and its value by His love.

Theologically stated, in God being, knowledge, and love are one, as the three Persons of the Trinity are one. God's being IS knowledge and love, and God's knowledge and love ARE His being. That is why what God knows and loves IS. God's act of creating a thing, God's act of knowing a thing, and God's act of loving a thing are the very same act. Only our mind divides that act into three, as a prism divides unitary light into various colors.

Time is also like that prism, dividing up, for us, the single timeless act of God, the act by which He creates, knows, and loves all things, into many acts, one before the other, in time. When we speak of His knowledge and love creating the world in time, "in time" here modifies the noun "the world", not the verb "creating". This act of creating, whose object is in time, is a kind of reflection of the act (or action or activity) that He does in eternity (timelessness), in which He "begets" the Son and, with the Son, "spirates" the Spirit. The Son IS His knowledge, His Word, His Logos; and the Spirit IS His love, Their love. Their being is not *prior* to His knowing and loving; their being IS His knowing and loving, which are so real that they eternally become (or rather timelessly are) two distinct Divine Persons.

This high and palmy Trinitarian mystery is the key to this simple psalm. *Why* are the godly blessed? Because God the Father knows them; and He knows them because He knows their "way", which is Christ ("I AM the way"). He knows them because they are "in" Christ. And whatever God knows is real and therefore blessed with goodness and truth and beauty, with eternal life and joy, while what He does not know is not. Thus He says to the godly: "Come, ye blessed.... I knew you before the foundation of the world", while He says to the ungodly, "I never knew you." The most threatening word one can hear from his earthly father, as from his Heavenly Father, is, not "I hate you", but "I do not know you." We are blessed because we are known, and we are known because our "way" is known ("the LORD knoweth the way of the righteous"), and our way is known because our "way" is Christ, and we are "in" Christ.

That is the good news. There is also bad news. There is an alternative. There is Christ and Antichrist, being and nothing, good and evil, godliness and ungodliness, in and out, life and death. He says to all of us what He said to His chosen people through his greatest prophet, Moses: "I call heaven and earth to record this day against you, that I have set before you life and death, blessing and cursing: therefore choose life" (Deut 30:19). Life is choice; that is why life is dramatic.

Ultimately, this "blessing" and "curse" mean Heaven and Hell. This psalm is ultimately about eschatology. If there is no Hell, there is no salvation from it, and "salvation" becomes as meaningless as "salvation" from little green men in flying saucers. Heaven is then simply taken for granted. Only if there are two ways, not one, is life a drama. Only if there is night do we enjoy day; only if there is winter do we enjoy summer, only if there is fear do we enjoy relief. All are dramatic contrasts. God does not save us from falling INTO suffering and even sin; He saves us OUT of it.

In the King James Version, the last word of the Old Testament (Mal 4:6) is "curse". The last word of the New Testament (Rev 22:20) is "Jesus". The meaning of life is this drama, this choice, this spiritual war.

Our age worships equality, and therefore it is undramatic and therefore bored, and that is why it seeks excitement in war, in violence, in sexual aggression, and in sexual "transgressive" behavior of all kinds. Sexual orgasm, drugs, and war (killing or being killed) all bring us out of the gray, flat, safe world of equality into the life-or-death drama of standing on the brink of the volcano. They are all unconscious longings for what we are designed for: ecstasy, standing-outside-ourselves, losing our very selves in God.

One of the most popular false clichés of our age is that all roads lead to the top of the same mountain. We are not allowed to be "judgmental" among those roads. But reality is judgmental because its creator and designer, God, is judgmental. He cannot help it: truth cannot help judging falsehood as false; light cannot help judging darkness as dark; sight cannot help judging blindness as blind; beauty cannot help judging ugliness as ugly; goodness cannot help judging badness as bad; and reality cannot help judging unreality as unreal. All evil is judged just by being what it is. Not all roads lead up the mountain; some lead down. Not all roads lead to Rome: you cannot get there from Naples by walking south, only north.

If gods were many, it might well be true that all roads are equal and that we should not be "judgmental". For if roads are many—as many as there are gods—then perhaps all are ultimately the same in value and in ultimate destination. Many gods, many roads. But precisely because God is one, because there is only one absolutely absolute absolute, therefore the roads are only two: toward the One Goal and away from it. If gods were many, then "away from one god" (Zeus, e.g.) might well be "toward another god" (Hera, e.g.). But because God is one, the roads are only two. And therefore life is infinitely dramatic. It is all or nothing. Because God is not *a* god, it is *God or Nothing*. (Cardinal Sarah's great title says it all.)

Those who come to the United States, Canada, or northern Europe from more "primitive" countries like Greece, Russia, or Arabia often comment on our lack of passion, heroism, and courage. (See, e.g., Solzhenitsyn's great 1978 Harvard commencement address.) We lack what Kierkegaard called "infinite passion" because we have lost the very category of the infinite, outside of theoretical mathematics. The startling (to us) "good news" of this psalm is that there is Something which demands infinite passion.

The Twenty-Third Psalm

"The LORD is my shepherd"

This psalm is almost everyone's favorite. Every other psalm is known as "Psalm 1" or "Psalm 19" or "Psalm 51", but this one is never known as "Psalm 23". That is too impersonal, too mathematical. It is not "Psalm 23" but "the Twenty-Third Psalm".

But it is almost always misunderstood.

Not all misunderstandings are intellectual. That is a typically academic superstition. Some misunderstandings are emotional. This psalm is rarely misunderstood intellectually (e.g., by taking its analogies and images literally), but it is misunderstood emotionally not only occasionally but *usually*. Even more surprising, it is the same misunderstanding both on the part of those who love it (who are the many) and by those who hate it (who are the few). It is misunderstood by most believers in the same way Nietzsche, the greatest and most passionate enemy of Christianity, misunderstood Christianity in general: as "tame", "sweet", "soothing", or "relaxing".

The misunderstanding common to both its friends and its enemies is the forgetting of its first and most important term, which colors the whole rest of the psalm. The term is "The LORD", "Adonai". This is the word Jews use as a substitute for one that is even more formidable (that is

54

the right word: not just "great", but "formidable"); the word that is so formidable that it dare not ever be spoken: the sacred Tetragrammaton (four-letter-word without the vowels), YHWH; the word that, when Christ spoke it (Jn 8:58), provoked murderous anger and a failed attempt at stoning and, later, a successful attempt at crucifixion. Is there any such word today? Any such passion?

The LORD is my shepherd;

The misunderstanding is that this is a sweet, soft, soothing, "sissy psalm". It says that "my lord is *a shepherd*", and that feels nice. It seems to change something fearful into something nice, to reduce lordship to shepherding, to caring, or "sharing and caring". Up leaps onto the screen of the unconscious a big yellow smiley face. God is Mister Rogers, and the Church is Mister Rogers' Neighborhood.

No, it does not say that. It says almost the exact opposite. It says that my shepherd is *the Lord*, YHWH. It changes something nice into something formidable. It does not reduce the Lord to a shepherd but elevates shepherding to Lordship, caring to adoration. It does not say: "Your Lord may be formidable, fearful, and terrible, but mine is nice. He's just my shepherd, and I am sheepish." Rather, it says: "Your shepherd may be a nice man, but mine is the Lord of the universe!" The biblical image of God is not a happy face with the color of a pale yellow post-it note, but a burning bush. For "our God is a consuming fire" (Heb 12:29). Granted, the bush is not consumed, but that adds to the formidability: the fire never goes out. Even after it consumes and burns to death all our sins, it burns in our heart as the fire of divine love and life. We are destined to become that burning bush which is not consumed: we are not consumed, but all our sins are.

The fire is divine love, of course; but divine love is a volcano, not a heating pad. God is a lion, not a pussycat. As Rabbi Abraham Joshua Heschel said, "God is not nice, He is not an uncle. God is an earthquake." *That* is the One who chooses to become my shepherd. It is like an elephant taking care of mice.

The Bible often says that "the fear of the LORD is the beginning of wisdom" (Ps 111:10; Prov 1:7; 9:10). This is not servile fear, the fear in a slave toward a cruel master, but filial fear, the loving son's fear of offending and disappointing his father. It is also the fear that is wonder and adoration toward One who is infinitely greater than we can imagine. "Perfect love casteth out fear" (1 Jn 4:18), but the true love of God begins in the true fear of God. The fear of the Lord is not the *end* of wisdom—that is what the love of God is—but it *is* the beginning. If we cease to fear God, we will cease to love Him. If we cease to know His fearsomeness, we will soon cease to know His condescension and humility in loving us spiritual fleas. Only because this is the high and holy God who condescends to shepherd us and even to die for us, is Christianity amazing and paradoxical rather than merely comforting and nice. Niceness is not amazing. The two halves of the Christian paradox, "Lord" and "shepherd", are inseparable parts of a "package deal".

Since God is both the infinitely powerful Lord and the infinitely loving Shepherd, the shock can go either way. If one begins with the God of power ("Almighty God"—it is almost His middle name), the love is the shock. For power is not usually loving. In fact, "all power tends to corrupt"—but not here. And if one begins with the God of love, it is the power that is the shock. Love does not seem powerful—look at the paradigm of divine love dying on the Cross—but it is in fact the greatest power in the universe. Love often looks sissified—but not here. Either way, the juxtaposition is a shock.

Machiavelli chose power over love and, therefore, fear over love, for he argued that "it is better to be feared than to be loved, if you cannot be both", for men will love you when *they* wish, but they will fear you when *you* wish. How could it be different with God? It is a shock. If we are not shocked by this verse, we are not really listening to its "good *news*". We are misusing its alarm clock as a sleeping pill, its trumpet call as a lullaby.

If we add a third divine attribute to infinite power and infinite love, namely, infinite wisdom, we are pushed, we are forced, we are compelled to a conclusion that is at once unbelievable and undeniable: that "all things work together for good" (Rom 8:28) for those who choose to allow this God to be their Father and Shepherd. For if God wills only good to those He loves, has the power to attain everything He wills, and knows infallibly what will in the long run be the very best for His beloved, then this is the only possible answer to the problem of evil: that, as Aquinas says, quoting Augustine, "God would not allow any evil in any of His works unless His omnipotence and goodness were such as to bring good even out of evil." It is ironclad logic from the divine Logos, however shocking it may seem to our feeble, feathery minds. For, as God reminded Saint Catherine, "I'm God; you're not."

I shall not want.

So the second sentence in the verse, "I shall not want", is a conclusion that follows with logical certainty from the first, "The Lord is my shepherd", as a conclusion follows a premise in a syllogism.

For "I shall not want" does not mean "I shall not desire" or "I shall not wish"; rather, it means "I shall not need." It does not mean "I shall not ever kvetch and complain, I shall not ever feel abandoned and ignored, I shall not foolishly desire that God would do things differently." It means "I shall in fact lack nothing good." As Augustine says, "He who has God has everything, even if he has nothing else; and he who has everything else but not God, has nothing; and he who has God plus everything else, has nothing more than he who has God alone." If that is not so, God is not God. He is just *a* god. Our muddled minds really worship *a* god most of the time. That is why God put the first commandment first.

> He maketh me to lie down in green pastures:

Every one of the rest of the sentences in this psalm is an example, or an image, of its central point, which is made in verse 1.

The first image is lying down in green pastures. Lying down, as distinct from running, walking, hiding, jumping, or standing, is the posture of total trust and submission for us, as with most mammals. (Think of your dogs and cats.) Lying down is also the posture of rest. The pastures are green, soft, and alive rather than brown, dry, and dead.

"He maketh me to lie down" means, of course, not "He forces me to lie down" like a bully with a weapon, but that "What He does and is, like a guarding angel, allows me to lie down." Lying down is an expression of trust.

> he leadeth me beside the still waters.

If you watch shepherds in the Holy Land today, you see why David, who was himself a shepherd, says "He leadeth me." In most parts of the world, shepherds, like their dogs, are *behind* their sheep, barking at their heels. The shepherd of this psalm, however, goes first, *leading* the sheep, who follow out of trust rather than run out of fear. They seek, rather than flee, the shepherd's presence. The "fear" of the Lord that we spoke of earlier is not the "fear" that repels them from Him, the fear of the slave, but the fear that attracts them to Him, the fear of a child.

Why are the sheep who follow in the rear not afraid of the wolves, who are their natural enemies and who want to turn them into food, as demons want to do to us? To answer this question, listen to the One whom David here unknowingly symbolizes and foretells: "I am the good shepherd: the good shepherd giveth his life for the sheep" (Jn 10:11).

This also explains why He leads the sheep rather than following them: "The sheep follow him, for they know his voice" (Jn 10:4). They know Him because He knows them: "I am the good shepherd, and know my sheep, and am known of them" (Jn 10:14). "The sheep hear his voice: and he calleth his own sheep *by name*, and leadeth them out" (Jn 10:3, emphasis added). This "knowledge" is personal, concrete, and individual (*connaître*, *kennen*), not scientific, abstract, and general (*savoir*, *wissen*). Our Lord is our Father, not our boss, and His Son is our Shepherd, not our CEO. CEOs are not lovers or saviors.

Sheep instinctively fear moving waters (rivers, streams, even brooks) because they cannot swim, and their heavy coats, when wet, drag them down to drowning. But still waters are safe and life-giving to them. Their trust in their shepherd is so total that they do not fear any place their shepherd leads them, not even "the valley of the [mere] shadow of death". Why? Because of the infallible logic of verse 1.

He restoreth my soul:

One "restores" only something that is lost, taken away, or damaged. All is not well with the soul (the life) of these sheep: they need "restoration"—in other words, salvation. What did we lose in Eden? Only Heaven, God, our true identity, life, bliss, wisdom, virtue, self-control, freedom, happiness, peace, joy, faith, hope, love, truth, goodness, and beauty, of which we have now only the beautiful but broken shards and precious but pale images. And from what do we need to be saved? Only Hell, Satan, death, misery, folly, sin, addiction, slavery, war, sorrow, mistrust, despair, hate, lies, evil, and ugliness. That is all. A minor little restoration job.

This does not apply to literal sheep, of course: shepherds do not restore their souls. For this one sentence, David moves from the poetic image to the literal thing. This non-image reminds us that these images are not just a poetic escapist fantasy. They are true. Poetic images and analogies can be as importantly true as literal words. Both the literal words and the symbolic images in the psalm point to real things, in fact, the most real things of all: human souls, persons, free wills, rational minds, human lives, ultimately eternal life.

For the rest of the psalm, the poet will mix poetic images and literal statements. It is not thoughtless sloppiness but deliberate strategy. The very first verse set the tone for the mix: God is not a literal shepherd, but our want (need) is literal want.

> he leadeth me in the paths of righteousness for his
> name's sake.

Righteousness is called a "path". The image of life as a road, the fundamental image of Psalm 1 and of most of the world's great epics, is repeated here. The invisible (righteousness) is imaged by the visible (a path).

God invented the whole material universe for this purpose: to reveal Himself, to reveal spirit through matter and through our material senses, to our spiritual mind. "The heavens [and the earth] declare the glory of God" to our minds through our bodies and their senses.

The truth of the poetic image is attested to by the fact that this "road" or "path" is by far the single most popular image for human life in all the literature of the world. Life is dynamic, not static; a drama, not a formula; a road on which we move ahead or back, up or down—the two "ways".

In order to move forward and upward toward "righteousness" (goodness), we need His leading. He goes first, His sheep follow. Christ "the Way" walks first on the road. He *is* the road. He reveals the meaning of life. He *is* the meaning of life.

He reveals the two things we need to know because they are the two persons we cannot ever avoid for one second either in life or in death: He reveals who God is and who man is because He is both perfect God and perfect man.

Notice also that it is a personal "path", not an impersonal superhighway or railroad track. Although we are saved into a community, the Church, we are not saved en masse, because we did not sin en masse, and we do not choose to believe, to hope, or to love en masse. Asked why she did not rely on large, rich, and powerful global organizations, Mother Teresa replied that she wanted to do Jesus' work in the same way Jesus did it, "one at a time".

We need to be careful with that word "righteousness". Subconsciously, we tend to think of it as something cold and legalistic because it sounds so similar to "*self*-righteousness", which is its polar opposite. Similarly, we associate "goodness" with "goody-goodyness". But it means simply goodness, which, in the last analysis, is simply goodwill, the will to the best good of the other, which, in the last analysis, is simply love.

Love is very easy to understand and very hard to live. We pretend not to understand it, we make it hard to understand, we "nuance" it, we relativize it, we add ifs and ands and buts—why? To try to make it easier to live, since the real thing is *not* easy to live. So we take what is easy to understand and hard to live and make it hard to understand and easy to live.

God leads us in the paths of righteousness "for his name's sake". What does that mean? It does not mean "for selfish motives". God has no selfish motives. He is not an egotist. When He tells us to be unselfish, He preaches to us in time only what He practices in eternity: the Father, Son, and Spirit eternally give themselves away in unselfish love to each other.

So what does "for his name's sake" mean, then? It means "for the sake of revealing His name (i.e., His personality, His nature) to us so that we can know Him". It is for our profit, not His. Our knowing, loving, and following Him cannot add an atom of worth to Him, only to us. Yet it pleases Him, as a baby's learning to walk pleases a parent. He cares, even though He is not in any need. He cares *for* us, like a shepherd, because He cares *about* us, like a lover.

> Yea, though I walk through the valley of the shadow
> of death, I will fear no evil:

The first word ("yea") is an intensifier, like "indeed". For death is intense. Nothing is more fearful than death (both physically and spiritually), because in death we lose not just some things in life but everything. Only if we have two kinds of life can we survive the death of one kind. What does that mean, "two kinds of life"? It means two things:

first of all, it means that if we have been baptized and have faith, we have not only natural life but also supernatural life (the life of grace, the sharing in God's life); and it means also that, within natural life, we have the life of the body and the life of the soul. Bullets and cancers cannot kill souls. Supernatural death is the death of the soul; natural death is the death of the body.

Both deaths are fearsome and suggested by the Psalmist's image of this life as "the valley of the shadow of death". It is a powerful and terrifying image. Think of the Mines of Moria, Shelob's lair, or the Cracks of Doom in Mordor in *The Lord of the Rings*. A valley hems you in and blocks most of the sunlight. A shadow also blocks your light. It also means that there is something unseen that casts the shadow. That something is death.

This is jarring: What is death doing as a character in the comforting drama of the good shepherd? The answer is that death is the test case for this hopeful and comforting psalm. If this shepherd is the Lord, He can take care even of our fear of death, and if He can do that, He can take care of anything. And He can take care of the fear of death only because He can take care of death itself. He proved that in His Resurrection.

We know what death is, but what, exactly, is "the valley of the shadow of death"? Great suffering? War and battle? Life-threatening disease? (*Birth* is a life-threatening disease. It is always fatal. No one gets out of this place alive.) It is not any one of them but all of them, and more. It is an utterly realistic image for human life on earth. As Buddha perceived in his "first noble truth", "to live is to suffer." And life is so fragile that death can come instantly at any moment. We have an enemy that seeks to kill us, and eventually he has the last word, it seems, at least over our bodies. Life is a war of defense against that aggressor, and in this life victory is only temporary. That is why Tolkien's epic is so realistic, and not escapist fantasy. The Shadow's defeat in this life is only temporary. We cannot kill the Shadow forever; it is immortal. As far as physical life is concerned, our defeat is guaranteed. The best soldiers of life cannot defeat the soldiers of death. The only possible victory has something to do with "the paths of righteousness". We find ourselves in the middle of a battlefield, and the battle is between the "valley of the shadow of death" and "the paths of righteousness".

But because of these "paths", the "valley" does not have the last word. There is evil, and it seems stronger than good. There is death, and it seems stronger than life. There is darkness, and it seems greater than light. The psalm does not ignore this data. But there is more data: there is the shepherd. The shepherd is the Lord. (Remember that first verse!) The Lord of life is stronger than the Lord of death.

> for thou art with me; thy rod and thy staff they comfort me.

Few words are more wonderful than the word "with". The most important thing we can do for each other in life, especially when life is at the point of death, is to be *with* each other. It is the aim of love: withness, intimacy, unity. To be human is to be with; to lose withness is to lose humanity. That is probably what Hell is: total loneliness. One of the saints (I forget which) says that he does not believe there is physical fire in Hell because that would ease the total loneliness there and would bring us out of ourselves, if only in pain and terror.

Withness is what we need and (if we are wise) what we most want and love because it is the nature of ultimate reality, the nature of God. God is not alone. God is with God:

"the Word was with God, and the Word was God."
God could not be love if God were aloneness rather than
withness. If God were only one Divine Person, He could
be only one-who-loves, not complete love itself; and He
could not be even that until He created other persons to
love. "God is love" and the doctrine of the Trinity logically imply each other.

When one we love is in pain, fear, sin, or the process
of dying, we can be with him in that trial, and that is the
very best thing we can do for him. We cannot take away
his pain, fear, sin, or dying.

But God can.

His "rod" and "staff" are His weapons. Whatever they
are—words, deeds, saints, angels, miracles, sacraments, or
grace (and all of these are good candidates for what the rod
and staff symbolize)—the fact that they are His is the salient
fact that takes away all fear.

God is love, and love fights. Love has weapons, because
love has enemies. This is true of God's love as well as ours.
The difference is that we often lose the fight, but God never
does. That is why these weapons of war "comfort me".

His strongest weapon is made of wood. It is a Cross.
The Cross is a sword, held at the hilt by Heavenly hands
and plunged into the heart of darkness and death with the
message, "Death, thou shalt die!"

Thou preparest a table before me in the presence of mine
enemies:

What a shocking image! We are on a battlefield, and our
formidable enemies are demons from Hell who lust and
salivate after our eternal souls. If these enemies are only
myths and not real, then Christ and Scripture and the
Church and all the saints are fools or liars. And right here

on the battle plain in plain sight of our enemies, Hell's greatest warriors, our Shepherd serves us a gourmet dinner! He taunts them. "He that sitteth in the heavens shall laugh: the LORD shall have them in derision" (Ps 2:4). For even though these evil spirits from Hell are so formidable and powerful and terrifying, the Psalmist does not fear them, because the Shepherd is with him. Compared with us little hobbits, our enemies look like wizards or dragons. But compared with Him, they look like mice, and He is an elephant.

This verse is not a prophecy of Heaven but a description of earth, of this life. Battles, battlefields, and enemies will not be in Heaven. This verse is about the present, not the future. Right now, we are sitting down in this battlefield at a banquet table, observed by our jealous and salivating enemies. And what are the foods and drinks that we are being served by this Lord who has been our shepherd and who has now become also our chef and waiter and servant? The answer is: Every single thing and event in our lives. The table's label is Romans 8:28.

thou anointest my head with oil;

This "anointing" is an Old Testament sacrament. The same Hebrew word is used for the Messiah, which literally means "the anointed one". Anointing is a prophecy. It means: "You will be the King/Queen." Each of us is to be a king or a queen. This is another incredible surprise. But God makes no mistakes.

But over what are we to be ruler? Our lives. We are to rule over everything once we let God rule over ourselves. Not other people; they are also to be kings and queens, not subjects. The things in our lives that now rule over us are to be deposed and made subject to us: the evils, the neutrals, and the goods, everything from sins to smart-phones to symphonies.

And there are many such things, probably more today than ever before. As our technology has spectacularly multiplied, so have our powers and, therefore, also our misuses of power, our sins. It is ironic and significant that we feel less powerful individually today than ever before, even though we are far more powerful collectively than ever before. God will clear up this complex problem with a single stroke. God declares that we are to be the rulers, not the servants, of all the good things that now enslave us and addict us, whether these are our powers, our stuff, our responsibilities, our jobs, our recreations, our friends, our relatives, our employers, our employees, or (first of all) ourselves.

God is here placing us on the throne of our own lives. He will do that to us only if we do it to Him first. Only when we get down off the throne and let Him sit there will He pick us up and set us there with Him.

my cup runneth over.

Paradoxically, once the power of the enslaving complexity of our lives has been broken by our kingly and queenly anointing, once we are freed from the slavish syndrome of "too much", we find a "much" that is not enslaving but empowering. Before this, "the world is too much with us", and we are crushed by its weight; but when God is with us and is our whole world, the "too much" that we no longer *need* becomes a plus, a blessing. We cannot have too much of God. For God is truth, good-ness, beauty, peace, and joy, while the world is always a mixture of these things with lies, evils, uglinesses, wars, and sorrows.

The "cup" here is the self, the single human self, the "I". That self is not big enough to contain all the joy that God pours into it, so that this overflow of joy must be shared. That is why the love of God always overflows into love of neighbor. God put the first great commandment first and the second second because God will always send you to your neighbor, but your neighbor will not always send you to God.

And these spiritual joys multiply when shared, unlike the material things of the world, which divide when shared. For material goods cannot occupy the same material place at the same time, but spiritual goods can. The more money or power we give, the less we have left. But the more truth, goodness, beauty, peace, or joy we share, the more our own share of them increases. This is a concrete fact of experience, not an abstract, preachy ideal. It is certain; it is provable in the laboratory of life. Give yourself away; it always makes you bigger.

Mother Teresa of Calcutta loved to say that "God cannot be outdone in generosity."

> Surely goodness and mercy shall follow me all the
>   days of my life:
> and I will dwell in the house of the LORD for ever.

David says "surely", not "hopefully". He is sure of this radically joyful truth. How can he be so sure? Not by an impersonal logical proof. We often make mistakes in our reasoning, even in simple matters like addition. Nor is it by a psychological feeling, however strong, for feelings are only subjective, and we know they often deceive. This surety comes only from a personal knowledge of the Shepherd, the knowledge that comes only from religion, i.e., lived relationship, interaction, the struggle to obey God's will and the honest prayers of faith, hope, adoration, thanksgiving, confession, repentance, intercession, and petition. Theology teaches us *what* God is; only prayer and the moral life teach us *who* He is. The object of his surety, or certainty, is not an idea but a Person. David "knows" (*wissen*) this because he knows (*kennen*) Him. The object of his faith is not first of all a proposition (e.g., "God exists" or "God is good") but a Person ("I AM"), just as the object of his obedience and love is not first of all a Law but the Lawgiver.

So that is David. What about you?

David also knows himself and his sins well enough to know that mercy must be added to justice in God in order to have this assurance in David. Justice is not the maximum but the minimum, the beginning. Old Testament Jews are constantly pleading to God for justice, and this is right, especially in matters of war and global politics; but when it comes to his own unique relationship to God, David is not so foolish as to ask for justice. Though David was "a man after God's own heart", a saint, yet he was also a sinner, even on at least one occasion a very great sinner (see Ps 51). To ask for justice is to ask for damnation. (If you doubt that, you do not know either who God is, what justice is, or what you yourself are.) To ask for Heaven is to ask for mercy. Let us never make the disastrous mistake of letting the object of our faith and hope be our own character and merits; it must be only the character of God, and not first of all His justice but His mercy. Let us be at least as wise as the Prodigal Son, who on his return hoped, not for his father's justice, but for his mercy—and got it, multiplied.

Since God is unchangeable, His mercy never changes even when our deservingness of it does. Therefore, David is sure that this mercy will follow him "all the days of my life", and since life extends beyond death, that it will also follow him forever in that "house of the LORD" that is Heaven, of which the earthly "house of the LORD", the great temple in Jerusalem, is a mere shadow or symbol.

In the true "house of the LORD", we will not just continue to live, but for the first time truly live. Our earthly houses, whether this means our present bodies or our present temples, are always shadowed by death, in this "valley of the shadow of death". The life of Heaven is to this life what a living person is to a ghost, what waking is to a dream, what morning is to night, what sight is to blindness, what the sun is to a candle.

Only the Lord can shepherd us there.

Psalm 51

"Have mercy upon me"

A boring but brief remark about why I put this psalm next in order.

The order of the 150 psalms in the Bible is not topical. The Psalter is divided into five "books", the first two of which are classified as David's. Thus, at the end of Psalm 72, we have the words "The prayers of David the son of Jesse are ended." (Yet a number of psalms after 72 are also labeled "a psalm of David".) Each of the five "books" mixes themes randomly, so the order we have (1 through 150) is nothing more than the numerical counting of these randomly ordered psalms. The only obvious order is that Psalm 1 is the gateway and foundation to the other 149, and Psalm 150 is their summary.

I have ordered my twelve chosen psalms by a loose but natural spiritual or psychological progression. We begin with the spiritual foundation or presupposition of all of them (Ps 1) and then proceed to the most loved and intimate one (Ps 23), since love is the point of it all, and then to the sinner's favorite psalm, Psalm 51. For it is in light of the tender and beautiful intimacy and trust of Psalm 23 that sin stands out most clearly and most horribly. Sin betrays that trust and abandons that intimacy and love.

The Jews had a much more acute notion of sin than the pagans did because they had a much more acute sense of God's closeness and intimacy, as well as a sense of His will and love. These two ideas were joined in the idea of the "covenant", the spiritual marriage between themselves and God. As a human covenant of marriage is more than a concept of the mind or a law for the moral will, but is a whole-self relationship of the heart, so the religious covenant with God was more than mental (though it did involve belief) and more than moral (though it did involve obedience).

Thus the two most fundamental, and fundamentally different, ways of life for the Jews were not faith as belief versus doubt as unbelief, for faith was more than intellectual belief. ("Thou believest that there is one God; thou doest well: the devils also believe, and tremble"—Jas 2:19.) It was not the relation between a mind and a truth but between a person and a Person. Nor were the two ways sin versus virtue, for sin was more than just moral vice; it was breaking that intimate faith-relationship (i.e., the fidelity-relationship) with God. Thus Saint Paul says that "whatsoever is not of faith is sin" (Rom 14:23). Those are the two opposites.

So only one who appreciates the greatness of faith, as the covenant intimacy with God, can appreciate the greatness of sin, as the breaking of that covenant. Only one who appreciates the greatness of marriage can appreciate the tragedy of divorce. That is why the saints take sin more seriously than anyone else: not because they are such pessimists, but because they are such optimists: they believe our designed end is nothing less than spiritual *marriage* to God.

That makes possible what Kierkegaard calls "the infinite passion" and what our culture calls "fanaticism". In our modern world, especially in Canada and the United States, most people are simply "nice". They are neither great saints nor great sinners, simply because they are not great, not great of heart. We associate "great passion" only with homicidal maniacs and sexual predators, not with saints. The Bible has two kinds of personalities that neither post-Christian modernity nor pre-Christian paganism have: passionately great saints and passionately great sinners. Often, they are in the same person. David was a great saint. That is why he could be such a great sinner.

David's adultery with Bathsheba was not unusual; many men, in many societies, have similarly abused both their wives and their mistresses. But David was "a man after [God's] own heart". He was God's man. My closest childhood friend had the last name "Heerema". It is Dutch, and it means "The Lord's man". I always envied him his name.

David's sin, which he here confesses, for which he here repents, and for which he here pleads for God's mercy and forgiveness, is not only adultery but murder. (The story is found in 2 Samuel 11 and 12.) We may not be shocked at adultery, even from a saint like David, but murder? How could this happen in "God's man"?

The same way someone who becomes a drug addict can commit crimes he never committed before. Addiction blinds the mind. And lust is the most common and powerful addiction in history. Addiction shuts down the reason, which is the critic and censor of the passions, and turns it into rationalization. Reason is made to serve and obey the passions rather than the passions serving and obeying the reason. This is exactly what many popular modern philosophers (Hobbes, Hume, Mill, and Freud) say inevitably happens because it must happen and therefore ought to happen. (Yes, they actually say that! Check it out.)

The devil's strategy is very simple. It is like blocking a defensive player (who symbolizes the reason) in football or basketball or hockey to clear a path for your offensive player (who symbolizes the destructive passion to which you are addicted, whether sexual or any other). All the premodern moralists say that the greatest danger in lust is its harm to the reason. (The intuitive reason, the seeing reason, not the calculating reason.) This is not because they think of intellectual virtue as the most important thing but because they see that it turns the judge into the prisoner and the prisoner into the judge. It turns the horse into the rider and the rider into the horse.

> Have mercy upon me, O God, according to thy
>   lovingkindness:
> according unto the multitude of thy tender mercies
>   blot out my transgressions.

We have no choice about whether or not we die or whether or not we go to court to face God in the Last Judgment. What we do have a choice about is how we plead in this court. We can plead "innocent" and ask for justice, or we can plead "guilty" and hope for mercy. The first plan is absolutely the most stupid thing we can possibly do. It is spiritual suicide. Our *only* hope is to stand "under The Mercy". That means, for a Christian, under the Cross.

Our Judge is not like earthly judges. Earthly judges base their judgment on justice and on the character and actions of the judged. If God judged us by those two standards, no one could have any hope of Heaven. Our only hope is that God bases His judgment of us on His own character, not ours; and, within that, on His mercy rather than His justice. Thus David pleads that God use "the multitude of thy tender mercies" as His standard of judgment, and not either simply His justice or our transgressions.

He cannot compromise *any* aspect of His unchangeable, eternal character, so He has to find a way to reconcile both justice and mercy, which He did on the Cross, where the Great Exchange took place, so that Christ got the justice and we got the mercy. He could not ignore either of those two aspects of Himself, for mercy without justice is soft and squooshy, immoral and cheap, while justice without mercy is hard and unyielding, true but unendurable. David did not know (*wissen*) how God would reconcile His justice and His mercy in Christ, of course; but, like any good Jew, he knew (*kennen*) God, and he knew God's character, especially His mercy and His cleverness in finding a way to express it in a world of sin, to coordinate "the multitude of thy tender mercies" with the truth of justice and of "my transgressions". He knew those two things as his indubitable data: God's goodness, which included mercy as well as justice, and his own badness and transgressions.

That is where we all must begin, too—with this double data—if we are to have any hope at all. Only the combination of these two insights allows us to hope. If we deny God's mercy, we will get only what is left, His justice. And if we deny our sinfulness, we will not think we need His mercy and not ask for it, and then we will not get it, for a gift needs to be freely accepted as well as freely given.

Our transgressions are far more, and far worse, than we think. And God's mercies are also far more, and far greater, than we think. And only if the "far more" of His mercies is itself far more than the "far more" of our transgressions do we have ground for hope. And that is the case, for God's goodness is infinite, while our evil is only finite. No sin can be greater than God's mercy. Only our refusal to confess and repent and humbly plead for His mercy can block His mercy. However sick we are, the Great Physician can heal us if only we unlock the door of our pride and let Him come in.

That is why the Church puts the "Kyrie, eleison" at the very beginning of the Mass.

> Wash me thoroughly from mine iniquity,
> and cleanse me from my sin.

Sin has many dimensions. One is personal pollution, the presence of dirt, of darkness, of disease in us. Sin is to the soul what dirt or disease is to the body. (Disease is a better image than dirt because it is internal, not just external.) And the "catch-22" is that it is sin that prevents us from cleansing ourselves from sin because the hands with which we wash ourselves are dirty. "Physician, heal thyself." The doctor is himself diseased and reinfects himself with every attempt at self-healing. Thus pop psychology exacerbates our egotism in the very act of dealing with our egotism. We become proud of our humility. We trust in our humility instead of trusting in *God's* humility and condescension. And this is inevitable and inescapable, for it must be the sinful self that tries to conquer, forget, transcend, or overcome the self. But how can the self escape itself? It is a logical self-contradiction. We can escape the enemy without, but we cannot escape the enemy within, because we *are* the enemy within, and we cannot escape ourselves any more than we can escape God. We cannot pull ourselves up by our own bootstraps. We cannot climb out of the quicksand into which we have sunk. Only someone standing on the solid ground can pull us out. We cannot save ourselves any more than we could create ourselves. We need a Savior as much as we need a Creator. And we cannot deserve either one. For how could we deserve to be created before we were created? And how could we deserve to be saved from what we deserve if we were not deserving?

Another dimension of sin is the relational dimension. We have pulled the plug to God and no longer have the power to put it back. We have divorced ourselves from our divine Husband and no longer have His name or His authority. We have forged the chains of our bondage with the very strength of our freedom and no longer have the freedom to break those bonds. We have sold ourselves into slavery and have nothing left with which to redeem ourselves, no ransom money with which to purchase our liberty. We need a Redeemer. The leopard cannot change his spots; he can only paint over them and disguise them from others, and even from himself. David here refuses to do that.

> For I acknowledge my transgressions:
> and my sin is ever before me.

Sin is not just an act but a fact. The act of "transgression" may be past, but the transgressor is always present as the transgressor. Even if we could escape our past, we cannot escape our present. I think that is what David means by "my sin is ever before me." It is not that he is always thinking about sin. That is obsessive. It is that he admits that his sin is in fact always with him, whether he brings it to mind or not. The same self that lusted after Bathsheba, committed adultery with her, and arranged for her husband Uriah's murder is still present as David is praying. It is not just the actions but also the actor, that self, that sinful self, that he is presenting to God in his confession. But he is repenting it; he is presenting it for treatment, for a kind of death. He does not want God to "accept" it. He is not a Pharisee or a pop psychologist: he does *not* accept himself as he is, and he does not want God to accept him as he is. He wants God to forgive him and to change him. He wants God to take away his sin, not just his punishment. In abstract theological terms, he is asking for both justification and sanctification, for both forgiveness and transformation, for salvation from both the punishment and the sinfulness that deserves it. We do not address our Redeemer, in the Mass, as the Lamb of God "who takes away the *punishments* of the world" but He "who takes away the *sins* of the world".

God is adamant about the need for that whole treatment: "Be ye therefore perfect, even as your Father which is in heaven is perfect" (Mt 5:48). The treatment will not be completed in this life, but it must be begun in this life, in fact at this very moment, which is the only moment that is real, the moment called the present. Macbeth postpones it to "tomorrow, and tomorrow, and tomorrow". He is on his way to Hell. The most profound description of that play is that it is a psychology of damnation.

> Against thee, thee only, have I sinned,
> and done this evil in thy sight:

Wait a second here: David sinned against *Bathsheba*, whom he seduced, against *Uriah*, whom he murdered, and against all *Israel*, in becoming now their wicked king instead of their saintly king. How can David say to God that it was only against Him that he sinned? Is he denying or ignoring the social and human dimensions of sin?

Not at all. He knows, better than we individualistic and non-mystical moderns, that there are no "victimless crimes", that all sin has social consequences, and that there is a strong and invisible spiritual gravity that unites all men in both vice and virtue. Ancient peoples had a deep sense of *sobornost*, as the Russians call it. They understood that humanity was a single family and that all sins harm all in the family. That is why no one until modern times questioned

the fundamental datum of "Original Sin", for they saw the
human race as a tree, individuals as leaves on it, and the
sap (life) of the tree as one. It is we modern autonomous
individualists who have problems seeing that, especially if
we no longer see our ancestors and our children as essential parts of our identity.

Why, then, does David say he has sinned against God
only? For three reasons. First, David knows that just as
"all truth is God's truth" because He is Truth itself, so all
goodness is God's goodness because God is goodness itself,
and so all sins are sins against Him. Second, he knows
that all sins against His children are sins against their one
Father. Third, he knows that only the one God who is our
one Creator is also our one true Lawgiver and our one
true Judge.

> that thou mightest be justified when thou speakest,
> And be clear when thou judgest.

The word "that" here does not mean "in order that" or
"so that". It is not God's *purpose* or goal or desire that He
be justified when He speaks and clear when He judges.
He has no need to worry about His own perfection!
Rather, this is the *logical* "that". It means "it necessarily
follows that". What David is saying here is that there
is no more question of God's judgment being unjust
than of justice itself being unjust. There is in fact, and
in David's wise heart, no possible distinction between
justice itself and God Himself. God is not just just, God
is justice itself. But He is not just the abstract perfect Platonic Idea of Justice, as in the *Republic*. He is God! Yet
He is not one of the pagan gods. He is justice itself, as
well as mercy itself and love itself. That is why His judgment can never be unjust.

And David knows what God's (i.e., justice's) judgment of sin is. For He has very clearly told us that through Moses and the prophets.

> Behold, I was shapen in iniquity;
> and in sin did my mother conceive me.

This is what later theologians will call "Original Sin".

It does not mean our first actual sinful act or Adam's first sinful act. It is a state, not an act. Just as a singer is still a singer even when he is not singing, so a sinner is a sinner even when he is not sinning.

Nor does "Original Sin" mean that sex, biological conception, or motherhood is sinful. One might think that because Original Sin is inherited. But heredity is not merely biological; it is also spiritual or psychological. We inherit our whole human nature, body and soul, from our parents and ancestors.

Nor does "Original Sin" mean that infants without functional free choice can actually sin. Actual sins always presuppose actual, not just potential, freedom of choice. Functional free choice does not click in until sometime later than one and earlier than five. It is gradual, not sudden and all at once.

Original Sin is our innate *tendency* actually to sin. It means that there is no time in anyone's life when he is free from concupiscence, from instinctive selfishness. We pop out of the womb programmed to think "I want what I want when I want it." That is not theory, that is fact. The evidence for that fact is massive. Chesterton says that Original Sin is the only dogma of the Faith that can be proved simply by reading the daily newspaper. Dogmas are facts, not ideologies.

David is not putting forward this fact, this dogma, as an excuse. "I am a tyrant" is no excuse for tyranny. It is the opposite from an excuse: it enlarges rather than shrinks your personal responsibility, for it recognizes that you cannot be responsible for what you do without being responsible for what you are, since what you are (your character) is always both a cause and an effect of what you do. You might be excused for one tyrannical deed, but if tyranny goes down to the roots of your being, you are apparently hopeless. How can the leopard change its spots?

The answer is clear: He cannot. If Original Sin is fact #1, that is fact #2.

But God can change you. That is fact #3.

That is why David is praying rather than philosophizing, moralizing, or suggesting some practical self-improvement programs or some politics (any politics at all), even though he has the power of a king. Sin comes from the heart, and only the Creator can create a new heart in us, can put something of His own utterly unselfish and unsullied life into our stained, selfish souls.

> Behold, thou desirest truth in the inward parts:
> and in the hidden part thou shalt make me to know
>   wisdom.

If there is to be any hope at all, the first and most necessary thing is the honesty to admit the truth. This honesty, this will to truth in oneself, is the first part of wisdom. If there is to be any hope of a healing operation, the first necessity is light. God does not just desire truth, He demands it.

"Truth" here means not merely the philosopher's impersonal definition of it, something like "the mind's correspondence to objective reality". It is much more than that. The word is *emeth*, and it characterizes a person, not an idea. It also means "faith" or "fidelity", i.e., total trustability. God demands this *emeth*, this honesty, purity, authenticity, and integrity in the heart and will and mind as well as in actions. He demands what we do not have and cannot give to ourselves, though we can love it and choose it and accept it when God gives it to us by His terrible grace.

It is not "cheap grace". It demands everything. If the very self is to be transformed, the very self must offer itself for transformation, for death and resurrection.

To want that "truth", that *emeth*, that transformation, that "treatment", that heart surgery, as David does here, is to have learned the lesson of Psalm 1 (that there are only two options, two ways, two roads: toward God or away from God) and the lesson of Psalm 139 (that God knows you perfectly and your only choices are Yes or No to that fact: see the next chapter).

That treatment will happen if and only if two persons desire it: you and God. God already does desire it: that is said in the first sentence of this verse. (How could Truth Himself desire anything but truth?) If we, too, desire it, and insofar as we do, it will happen, God *will* make us to know this wisdom. He will enter us if only we open the door. ("Behold, I stand at the door, and knock: if any man hear my voice, and open the door, I will come in to him" [Rev 3:20].) But the lock is on the inside of the door of our will, not on the outside. He will not blow down our doors with the tornado of His Spirit, though He could. He will only gently enter our doors when we freely open them. This tornado is a gentleman. He is also our only hope. If you doubt that, you worship a false God.

> Purge me with hyssop, and I shall be clean:
> wash me, and I shall be whiter than snow.

This psalm is not something safe, like poetry, psychology, or theology, all of which can be done alone, in private. This is prayer, and prayer is a two-way conversation and a two-way action. God *answers* prayers! He "does stuff" to us! David knows that. David is asking God for "the treatment", fully realizing that God will give him what he asks for. Do not pray "Thy will be done" unless you mean it; otherwise, you will have to do a lot of ducking. If you pray for something God wants but you do not really want, you will find yourself in the middle of a large flock of ducks.

Hyssop is a fragrant, minty, blue herb. It is only a symbol here, for a physical fragrance "purges" only physical dirt, not spiritual dirt, and certainly not the person who has the dirt. But when God "purges" you, you yourself will change. True religion should come with a warning label. For God is a killer. He will kill things in you, as radiation kills cancer cells. His Spirit is a kind of real radiation. He is causal efficacy, not just formal accuracy. "The kingdom [rule] of God [in our lives] is not in word, but in power" (1 Cor 4:20: the word for "power" here is *dynamis*, from which we get the word "dynamite"). God is not an engineer with a slide rule or an attorney with a law book, but a surgeon with a scalpel. Heart surgery is a bloody thing.

Yet this spiritually bloody thing is also a cleansing thing. Of course, David did not know that it was the blood of the Messiah that had to be shed, that we had to be "washed in the Blood of the Lamb". But he did know that we needed to consent to God's operation, that we had to die to our self-will for God to purify us, and that it involved pain and sacrifice.

This "clean wash" of "white snow" that is our new nature falls from Heaven. But it falls gradually, throughout the winter of our lives. It does not happen all at once and immediately, like our technology's buttons. But once it begins, it will never end until we are totally clean. God will not stop until we are. Our justification was finished on the Cross, but our sanctification has barely begun. That is why there is a Purgatory: because, as George MacDonald says, God is "easy to please but hard to satisfy". He demands: "Be ye therefore perfect, as your Father which is in heaven is perfect" (Mt 5:48), and He will not let us go until we are.

He will not do it without our consent, and we cannot do it without His power.

> Make me to hear joy and gladness;
> that the bones which thou hast broken may rejoice.

When an animal's bones are misaligned, the surgeon sometimes has to break the bones in order to reset them. This is painful, yet a matter for rejoicing—like Purgatory. The very pain of seeing the full harm and horror of our sins, in Purgatory, will be a great joy to us because we will passionately *want* the painful cleansing we are getting. Saint Catherine of Genoa says that her mystical visions of Purgatory taught her these three things: (1) that there is far more pain in Purgatory than on earth because we see the full harm and horror of our sins and our distance from God; (2) that there is far more joy in Purgatory than on earth because this painful cleansing is what we will passionately long for; and (3) that the joy is far greater than the pain. For when we see God at the Last Judgment and are infallibly assured of our eternal salvation, God will "make me to hear joy and gladness", and it will make even the pains of Purgatorial bone-breaking something in which we "rejoice".

And both the breaking and the rejoicing begin in this life. If they do not begin here, they cannot end there. (I do not presume to speak to, or even about, great saints, who "skip" post-mortem Purgatory entirely because they let the divine surgeon not just begin but also finish the operation in this life.)

> Hide thy face from my sins,
> and blot out all mine iniquities.

This face-hiding and blotting-out are only metaphors, but some theologians, like Luther, take them for the definitive description of our justification, as if God put on blinders and deceived Himself, by hiding His eyes from the sight of our sins, or simply blotted out the record of our sins in His book, or His mind, without changing *us*. (This is called "the federal theory of justification".) Luther called the justified sinner "a pile of shit covered with snow". That is ridiculous—not because "shit" is a "bad word" (it appears in the Bible—see Job 20:7 and Phil 3:8), or because we are *not* a pile of shit, or because God's grace is *not* whiter than snow, but because God is Truth and does not hide anything and because God is a lover, not a lawyer.

When God's angel said that our Lord's name was to be "Jesus", i.e., "Savior", because He would save us from *our sins*, not just from His just punishments for them, he was saying that He was not like a bad bishop hiding his eyes from his priests' pedophilia, but like a loving and demanding surgeon insisting on getting all the cancer out of his patient. Thus, in the "Song of Songs", when He addresses us as "all fair" (twelve times!), it is not because He is hiding our sins from His knowledge but because they are really gone.

It is not a lie but a prophecy. Every sin will meet its necessary fate, which is eternal death in Hell. We are saved by being separated from our sins so that we do not share their necessary fate. We are separated from our sins by two things: objectively by Christ's atoning death and sub-jectively by our repentance and faith. This begins in this life and is completed in the next. If it does not begin in this life, it cannot be completed in the next. This world is a flower pot, and eternal life is a seed. If it is not planted here, it cannot be transplanted and perfected there.

In this larger context, we can affirm the truth of this psalm verse. It is true that God "hides" or turns His face away from our sins because they are gone; they go to Hell, while we go to Heaven. God does indeed blot our sins out, but when God blots them out, they are really out (completely in Heaven, gradually on earth), not still there but covered up. There is no cover-up in Heaven.

There are two reasons for that. One is simply that God knows everything. The second is that God's mind is not like ours: it does not conform to a preexisting truth by discovering it and correctly reflecting it. Rather, it cre-ates truths, like an artist, rather than discovering them, like a scientist. We exist, we have real being, because God knows us into real being—that is how He creates us—and in a similar way we are righteous, we have real righteous-ness, because God knows us into righteousness. It is all in the last verse of Psalm 1 (see pp. 46–51).

> Create in me a clean heart, O God;
> and renew a right spirit within me.

This is the central petition in this psalm, and the first word is the central word. It is the word "create" (*bara'*), the Hebrew verb that does not exist in any other ancient lan-guage, the verb that has only God for its subject because it speaks of the thing that only God can do: to create, not just to improve, heal, or straighten. We need more than improvement, healing, or straightening out. We need a new life, from an outside source. We are not merely mal-adjusted men who need to reform our actions; we are barren women who need to be impregnated with new life. That is the deepest reason why God is always pictured as male, not female, in Jewish, Christian, and Muslim holy books. (Of course, it is only a symbol; but it is a divinely revealed symbol.) To vary the image but not the point, we need not just heart surgery but a heart transplant.

This does not take away our human nature. It is "in me" that we ask God to create a new heart. We do not become another person, the old person being annihilated and the new one created out of nothing. It is not that radical a change. But almost. It is much more than an improvement in our quality, our virtue, our maturity, our wisdom, or our holiness. It is not an accidental change but a substantial change: something that did not exist before in us must begin to exist in us. It is not just a new life-style but a new life; it must be "infused" into us by God. Augustine says (and Luther, Pascal, and Kierkegaard all quote this) that for God to make a saint out of a sinner is a greater deed than for Him to make the universe out of nothing. For "nothing" did not resist His creation of the universe, but our old nature resists being "born again". As Pascal says, if you do not understand why God making a saint out of a sinner is a greater deed than creating something out of nothing, then you do not understand what a saint is or what a man is. You think either that a man is already a saint or that a saint is only a nice man.

This new life (*zoe* in Greek) is eternal. It is divine life. Since you cannot give what you do not have, only God can give it. Our new birth into this supernatural life (through faith and baptism, through "water and the Spirit") is our finite participation in the infinite life of God, in His "eternal life". Eternity is more than immortality or unendingness. That which is eternal has no beginning as well as no ending. So in the new birth, that which has no beginning (in itself) gets a beginning (in us). The same thing happens in our souls that happened in Mary's womb. The eternal, timeless God got a beginning in time. And that event has to happen again in each human soul if we are to live the life of Heaven.

What the angel said to Mary, he says also to us: "The Holy Ghost shall come upon thee, and the power of the Highest shall overshadow thee: therefore also that holy thing which shall be born of thee shall be called the Son of God" (Lk 1:35).

That is the Gospel, the nearly unbelievable Good News. That is what David prays for here, without of course understanding what he is praying for. Nor do we fully understand it, and we never will. Think of six steps on a step ladder: unbelievers, David, Mary at the time of the Annunciation, believers now, believers in Heaven, and God—each of the six in this list understands it better than the preceding ones.

Our end is not simply perfect human happiness. It is *theosis*, divinization. Christ the King is going through the world kissing frogs and turning them into princes.

> Cast me not away from thy presence;
> and take not thy holy spirit from me.

The first line here is what we deserve: to become castaways.

Being cast away from God is Hell. This is the very best definition of Hell, right here in this verse. All the rest, the fire and torture and demons, are extra additions or symbols and images of something far worse than they can represent. Once you understand Who God is, the loss of that Presence is so infinitely awful that no tortures can add anything to it. If you do not know that, you do not know God.

Traditionally, the pains of Hell are described under three headings: the pain of loss, the pain of the mind (despair), and the pain of the senses. The first is really the whole; the others are merely its expressions, its effects or consequences, or else only its analogies, images, or shadows. We may be more frightened by a monster's shadow than by the monster, but all the real evil is in the monster. The shadow adds nothing to the evil, only to our fear. ("There is nothing to fear but fear itself" is a really stupid saying!) Thus we may fear the subjective human pains of Hell more than the objective Godlessness of Hell that causes the pain, but the pain is only the effect or the shadow of the Godlessness. There cannot be more in the effect than in the cause.

What can we do to avoid this casting away? We can only pray. But we pray to The Mercy. Hope in The Mercy, not justice. Do not venture out unprotected into the burning sunlight of justice, or you will die. Remain Under The Mercy. It is absolutely our last, only, and final hope. Where is that Mercy? On the Cross. Cling to it, like the two Marys and John. It is the only life raft. The rest of the world is the Titanic.

Who is this Holy Spirit that David pleads be not taken from him? The Holy Spirit IS this joy-in-love, the love-joy, between the Father and the Son, just as the Son IS the truth and mind and word (*logos*) of the Father. Love and truth are the very essence of God, the very life of God, as human life is the life of man and sunlight is the light of the sun. Love-in-truth is the nature of God, as dogginess is the nature of a dog. That is why Christ can say "I AM the truth" and why Saint John can say not only that God is a lover, that God loves, but that "God IS love." Complete love is threefold: a lover, a beloved, and a loving: Father, Son, and Spirit.

The Spirit, like the Son, is sent by the Father. Like the Son, He is a gentleman: He does not enter the house of a human soul and life if He is not wanted, if we lock the door. God is a lover, not a rapist. God does not arbitrarily and autocratically "take away" His Spirit from us; His will is always to live with us and in us. Only *our* will, our sin, our No to Him, not His to us, takes away His Spirit.

Notice how the New Testament illuminates the Old here, as the Church's Trinitarian creeds illuminate the New Testament. It is like science: progress means that the new hypotheses, theories, and understandings are more complete because they more completely understand the original data. But the analogy is not perfect: unlike science, the Church does not discover and add any new data to divine revelation, to the original "Deposit of Faith" from Christ, but only interprets it, unpacks it. The new and final and complete data is Christ. It is Christ who is radically new; it is Christ who refutes the lament of Ecclesiastes (1:9) that "there is no new thing under the sun."

> Restore unto me the joy of thy salvation;
> and uphold me with thy free spirit.

Notice the implications of the word "restore". Only the saved can worry about losing their salvation. Only the married can be divorced. Only the faithful can become faithless. Only those who have tasted the fullness of joy can taste the emptiness of joylessness.

Notice also the connection between salvation and joy. We can be given joy by salvation from any misery or feared misery, but "the joy of *thy* salvation" is unique. It is "the joy without a (an earthly) cause". It is like peace "not as the world giveth" (Jn 14:27). It is a participation in the very joy of the Godhead, which is *agape*, the selfless, self-forgetful love between Persons. The "salvation" here is from sin, which is essentially the opposite of that *agape*, as divorce is the opposite of marriage and death the opposite of life. Thus "the joy of thy salvation" is not merely an *appendage* of salvation, a *consequence* of salvation. It is its very life. This joy is not an extra; it is the life itself. It is the very life of Christ. Christ is our joy (Jn 15:11), even if we do not feel it. Our feelings are not infallible.

In the previous verse, David pleaded with God not to take His Holy Spirit from him. His petition in this verse, "uphold me with thy free spirit", assumes that God has answered that earlier prayer. For a Spirit that has already been *withdrawn* from David cannot *uphold* David.

David also assumes that the Spirit is "free", a gift, a grace, not a just dessert. How do we know that? Our undeserv-ingness is a fact of experience, not just an assumption, but God's grace and mercy and forgiveness are a faith-assumption. They cannot be proved because they are not a necessity but depend on God's free choice. David also assumes that when the Spirit is given, He will "uphold" us, not crush us. These are all faith-assumptions. Unlike the Blessed Virgin Mary, we make many Assumptions, not just one. (Do not frown; it is not a puzzle, it is a pun.)

> Then will I teach transgressors thy ways;
> and sinners shall be converted unto thee.

You cannot teach what you do not know, because you cannot give what you do not have. David will teach oth-ers effectively only to the extent that he has been taught by God—taught to be humble and honest. Self-righteous, self-confidently comfortable, proud, Pharisaical teaching is the devil's work and produces the fruit of the devil, not of God. Diseased doctors only spread their disease. Conversions follow only when those who preach are converted.

But once you are converted to the Faith or reconverted and returned by confession and repentance, you will teach it, whether formally or informally, if not by what you say, then by what you are, which is much more effective. The arguments of philosophers and theologians are answerable; the lives of saints are not.

But if you *are* in the Faith, you *will* spread it, inevitably, like a good infection. And you will *want* to spread it, and teach it, because you love both your students and your subject. (Those are the two most important requirements for any good teacher.) Just as faith without works is dead, a faith that does not want to share itself with others, a faith that has no passion or pity for those who lack it, is also dead. A star that does not spread its light is a Black Hole.

Every Christian is a teacher with a mission, a missionary; because charity (*agape*) is not just a psychological motive but an ontological energy that Christians carry and that carries Christians. It is the very life of God in us. And as Thomas Aquinas says, the greatest act of charity that we can do for others is to lead them to the truth.

Not just to true propositions, but to the Truth, who is a Person. And that truth is not just the truth *about* love, but the truth that is love, just as that love is not just a love that is true, but a love that is Truth itself. That is what sinners will be converted to; that is the only thing worth converting to; and that is the only thing that has the power to convert.

When we spread the Faith, by deeds, words, or (best of all) both, that is the very life of God in us doing what it always does, inevitably spreading itself like light. When we reflect the Son-light, we are like mirrors reflecting sunlight. There is only one light, but many mirrors. We can reflect only what we receive, and we can receive only what we turn to. "Converting" means "turning". It is the turning of a mirror to the light. This is done in prayer, in worship, and in obedience.

> Deliver me from bloodguiltiness, O God, thou God
>   of my salvation:
> and my tongue shall sing aloud of thy righteousness.

David was responsible for Uriah's death. He was a murderer, for the murder weapon was not the Gentile spear that pierced Uriah's heart but those who put Uriah in the front of the battle knowing and desiring that he might die, and that was, first of all, the commanding officer and authority with the name of David. But most of us have never committed murder in that way, so our guilt is not "blood-guilt", it seems. We are guilty of many things but not of human blood, is that not so?

It is not so. All guilt is "blood-guilt", because the only way it could be atoned for was by God's blood. "Without shedding of blood is no remission" (Heb 9:22). All sins are sins of murder. Worse, all sins are guilty of God's blood. All sins contribute to deicide.

That is the baddest of bad news. Then comes the goodest of good news: that God will deliver us from that terrible guilt. We are guilty of God's death, and God delivers us from that guilt by that very death.

No one expected or understood that. No one. "Eye hath not seen, nor ear heard, neither have entered into the heart of man, the things which God hath prepared for them that love him" (1 Cor 2:9). That verse is true not only of our life after death but also of our life now.

And that good news is so good, that divine "righteousness" is so much greater than mere justice, that we cannot merely say it, but we must sing it, and sing it aloud. Wisdom knows, and instruction speaks, but love sings. This love is not merely a human emotion that is our *response* to God's love; it is the very air, or breath, or "Spirit", of God's love. (Those two English words, "air" and "spirit", are one and same word in both Hebrew [*ruah'*] and Greek [*pneuma*].) God uses us as His flute to play His music.

"To sing is to pray twice", said Augustine. We are saved by love, and love sings, and singing turns our hearts around. Music is the most powerful of all the arts in doing that.

Singing is by nature "aloud". If it is not aloud, it can still be singing "in your heart", but it will not "convert" anyone, not even from sorrow to joy, much less from sin to sanctity, if they do not hear it.

> O Lord, open thou my lips;
> and my mouth shall shew forth thy praise.

We hesitate to sing aloud, out of shyness or human respect or fear. But God can open our lips by first opening our heart. Thus, David's next question, answered by this verse, is: Where does this joy of open-lipped song come from? Ultimately, from God, the source of all joy. Before we can sing to others, we must sing to ourselves, and before we can sing to ourselves, God must sing to us, and in us, and thus through us. Our song is the echo of God's song; that is why it has power over our soul and over others. How often do we think to thank Him and praise Him for that gift, for the gift of music, which is the natural sacrament of joy?

Why do we not do that? Because He did not open our lips. Why did He not open our lips? Because we did not ask Him, we did not pray this verse.

So get on with it, already. Do it. Right now. Before you dare read another line. You have no idea how that delights Him. Lovers always increase their joy by sharing it and seeing their beloved in joy.

> For thou desirest not sacrifice; else would I give it:
> thou delightest not in burnt offering.
> The sacrifices of God are a broken spirit:
> a broken and a contrite heart, O God, thou wilt
>   not despise.

God delights in our joy, not in our sorrow or our suffering. Only insofar as our sacrifices give us joy, God delights in them. And they give us joy *only* when they come from love. But they give us joy (eventually) *whenever* they come from love.

This verse is not despising sacrifices and "burnt offerings", either literally or symbolically. (Symbolically, anything that is given up is "burnt" in that our possession of it is destroyed.) It is recommending and rejoicing in the one sacrifice that God does desire, which is the sacrifice of our hearts, the giving away of our hearts to Him. That is what love is: the heart giving itself to another, the self giving itself away, the self "donating" itself rather than merely donating one of its possessions, such as a sheep or a large check. (Of course, the self-giving can be *in* the sheep-giving or the check-giving. Or it can be withheld, with the sheep or the check acting as if it were a substitute for it.)

A heart that is broken is like an egg that is broken. You cannot eat an egg unless it is broken. Do you want to be useful to others? Do you want to be a "person-for-others"? Do you want to work for social justice and peace? Then let yourself be broken by God. For we are all like eggs. And, as C. S. Lewis says, you cannot just be a good egg forever; you must either hatch or go bad. To hatch, you must be broken. Paul Tournier says that the only heart that can be whole is a heart that has been broken.

Does this "brokenness" mean love or humility or being humbled by events or by other persons, or pain and suffering? All four; it is a package deal: love is not just a pleasant feeling; it is giving your heart away to another; and you cannot do that if you are not humble; and being humbled makes you humble; and being humbled is painful.

Next to pride, the thing that keeps us from this package deal that is the road to sanctity is fear. It is ironic, for fear of pain only adds to the pain. But it is foolish, because the pain that comes from being humbled, or humiliated, is only a pain to the ego and its pride. It is not a pain that can reach into the deepest part of the soul, the part that loves. It is only in the ego, which is the egg's shell. The pain is its cracking, but the bird inside (the heart, the place of deep joy, the self that loves) rejoices in the cracking. And so does the mother bird, who is God.

And you get His joy, not by fearing and avoiding pain, but by volunteering for life's most dangerous and daring mission, which is forgetting yourself altogether, mercilessly assassinating the chattering voice of caution in your inner calculator, and boldly bodysurfing into the impact zone of the wild whitewater wave of His love.

> Do good in thy good pleasure unto Zion:
> build thou the walls of Jerusalem.
> Then shalt thou be pleased with the sacrifices of
>   righteousness,
> with burnt offering and whole burnt offering:
> then shall they offer bullocks upon thine altar.

Perhaps all that David meant here was the literal physical sacrifices in the temple in Jerusalem; but the Holy Spirit

had something more in mind, something that those sacrifices were instituted to symbolize. Our "burnt offerings"
are not bullocks, the fire is not physical fire, and the altar
is not made of rocks. Our "burnt offerings" are our hearts,
which burn with the fire of self-giving love, and our altar
is Christ the Rock. We put ourselves and all our hopes
on that altar. That altar is very different from every other
sacrificial altar on earth. For whatever we sacrifice on that
altar, we get back. Nothing good that we sacrifice to Him
will be lost forever. That sacrificial death, and that one
only, is guaranteed resurrection.

Abraham received his beloved Isaac back, and we will
receive our bodies back, and also our souls, both in in-
conceivably improved condition, but only after we give
them up.

In the Old Testament, sacrifice was not just a gift, like a
Christmas present; it was a death. What was sacrificed was
killed. Most often, by fire. Is that what God wants for us?
Does He want us to cast ourselves into His "consuming
fire" (Heb 12:29), trusting that, like the burning bush, we
will not be consumed as our sins are consumed?

Yes. That is exactly what God wants. That is what is symbolized in the Old Testament sacrifices that He instituted.

But I thought God was love.

He is. That is why He is a consuming fire. Love is a
consuming fire, a death.

But that takes a lot of courage.

Faith gives you that courage.

But that takes an awful lot of faith.

No, it just takes faith. You either have it, or you do
not. Even mustard-seed-sized faith can move more than
mustard-seed-sized mountains. Faith is not a feeling that
comes in sizes, small and medium and large. It is like preg-
nancy: it either comes, or it does not. You either leap into

the fire that is God, or you do not. You either trust Him, or you do not. You either say "Yes" to His unutterably ecstatic and unutterably terrifying marriage proposal, or not. You are either pregnant with His life, or not.

But ... but ...

Stop thinking with your butt.

Psalm 139

"O LORD, thou hast searched me, and known me"

This psalm begins with a confession of the most non-negotiable fact in the world: that God is real and infallibly omniscient and knows absolutely everything in us. We have no choice about the fact, only about our reaction to the fact. And upon our reaction depends absolutely everything: life or death, Heaven or Hell.

There are great philosophers, notably Nietzsche and Sartre, who explicitly and deliberately choose Hell in order to avoid this fact. They do not call it Hell; they call it "freedom" or "the will to power". They would rather enter Hell singing "I Did It My Way" than entering Heaven singing "God's Way Is the Best Way." It is the world's most disastrous confusion. What they think is Hell—the Psalmist's love of this fact, the free accepting of this fact, the surrender to this fact, the welcoming of this fact—is in fact Heaven.

The fact is simply that God is God, that God created and designed each of us and therefore totally and absolutely knows us through and through, inside and out, upside and down. To hate this fact is Hell; to love this fact is Heaven.

God is light, God is Truth. To love truth is to love Heaven, for truth and light are what Heaven is made of. Consequently, to hate truth is to hate Heaven, to turn what is objectively (in itself) Heaven into what is subjectively (for you) Hell. The fact is nonnegotiable, unchangeable, and unavoidable. God cannot cease to be God, and therefore He cannot turn off His light, any more than the sun can. Heaven is that light, that truth, embraced. Hell is that Truth, too, but hated.

Truth is not just facts. "Facts" is a plural noun. "Truth" is a singular noun. Truth is not merely the knowledge of the correspondence between minds and facts. That is only a potentiality. Truth is an actuality, a being, almost a *thing*—like light. Truth is, ultimately, a Person: the only sane person who ever said, "I am ... the truth" (Jn 14:6).

O LORD, thou hast searched me, and known me.

David begins with the syllable "O". It is the sound that opens the mouth and the heart. It is the shape lips make when they begin to kiss. It enacts vulnerability. It is an expression of humility, for it is the admission of surprise. It also expresses admiration and amazement and even, at its height, adoration, at something incalculably greater than oneself. "Chummy" prayers that begin without such an "O" and proceed immediately to "Lord" run the risk of treating "Lord" horizontally rather than vertically, as one would treat one's equal: "Hey, there, Lord, here I am again. Nice to see you. Let's chat." The only chumminess with God that is honest and authentic comes after, and never before, the "O", the adoration. If it is surrounded and formed by the adoration, by the wonder, it is then more wonder, a second story on the edifice of wonder, rather than bypassing it; for there is a second great wonder in the fact that the Lord of the Universe should deign to search and know His flea that is me; that the Absolute Other should be absolutely intimate. But there is very little wonder that the mere divine Chum should be chummy. (God is a punster: "chum" is also the name fishermen give to extra little bits of inedible fish that they throw away or use as bait. The God who created the universe does not fit into a chum bucket.)

Neither the Jews of the Old Testament nor the Christians of the New ever used the word "Lord" (*Adonai* in Hebrew, *Kyrios* in Greek) for earthly, human lords like Caesar. Thus, the earliest Christian creed, that "Jesus Christ is Lord" (Phil 2:11), affirms Christianity's most distinctive and most offensive claim, the full deity of this man Jesus. This is why earthly tyrants fear and tremble before Christians until they apostacize and say "We have no king but Caesar" (Jn 19:15). Judaism and Christianity are the only two truly revolutionary forces in history, for when they say "Thus says the Lord", they invoke, not Caesar, but Caesar's Lord.

Face to face with this Lord, this light, all the shadowy ghosts in us instantly shrivel and die: all shamming and shilly-shallying and semblance and sophistry and swindling and sneakiness and shiftiness and shuffling; all faithlessness and fakery and forgery and falsity and fibbery and fabrication and phoniness and pharisaism; all dishonesty and dissembling and deception and delusion and deceitfulness and deviousness and doublemindedness and doubleheartedness and double-dealing; all posturing and posing and pretense and prevarication and perjury; all falsity and fraud and fudging and faking and feigning and flimflamming; all truthlessness and trickery and trumpery and Tartuffery; all bullshit and bluff and bunk and baloney; all hugger-mugger and hogwash and hype and hypocrisy; all mumbling, mealy mouthed, moldy mendacity. In fact, most of what we are. Look at all the words we have for it.

When Job met this Lord face to face, all the great and agonizing questions he had planned to ask Him died on his lips. All his ships sank like stones before they could cross that ocean. None of his problems were solved (that came only later); all of them were dissolved when he met God face to face.

That is the God David prays to in this psalm.

> Thou knowest my downsitting and my uprising,
> thou understandest my thought afar off.

We sit and we rise. We are not simply a sack of *skubala* (the Greek S-word), sitting on that great invention of Thomas Crapper. (That is his name. Look it up.) We also rise up from it. We go up and down like yo-yos. Instead of saying a simple Yes to God, like Mary, or a simple No to God, like Satan, we say both Yes and No. We say Yo. We are yo-yos.

God fully knows us and therefore fully knows both truths about us, our ups and our downs, our greatness and our wretchedness. Every great novelist, like Dostoyevsky, every great philosopher, like Pascal, and every great psychologist, like Christ, knows both.

And *understands* both. Mere knowledge can be from without, but understanding also knows the within. Understanding "stands under". Knowledge stands in the yard and looks into windows, but understanding stands under the roof of the house and lives in it. We trivialize this word "understanding" when we make it mean simply "compassion" or "sympathy", by which we usually mean more of a feeling in us than an insight into the other. Understanding means knowing every dimension of whatever or whomever is understood, both good and bad, light and dark, up and down. It is love that understands best. Love is not *added* to understanding. Love *is* understanding.

When the Psalmist says that God understands from "afar off", he means "from His transcendence"; but this does not mean "from without", from the yard instead of under the roof. He is present everywhere but contained and limited nowhere. Shakespeare is transcendent ("afar off") to his plays and to every character in them, yet he understands them best ("from inside") as their designer. God encompasses us—which is David's next point: that we do not encompass Him, but He encompasses us.

> Thou compassest my path and my lying down,
> and art acquainted with all my ways.

God "compasses" us in two ways. He "encompasses" us as Shakespeare "encompasses" everything and everyone in his plays: as our transcendent Creator and Designer and, therefore, not "from without" like an alien from a flying saucer (that is deism) nor "from within" like a soul in a body (that is pantheism). Both those imaginative pictures deceive because they reduce God to a creature who can be only in one place at a time. One creature is either within or without another creature because both are subject to the same laws of the same created order; but the transcendent Creator cannot be limited to creaturely alternatives.

The second way God "compasses" us is connoted by the word "path". He is our compass, our guide, our standard. He judges and gives meaning and direction to our journey. He is True North. Again this connotes transcendence, for one part of a system cannot judge the whole system. The compass point for the journey is not encompassed by the journey. The Knower of all things cannot be merely one of those things known, any more than the judge can be one of the prisoners on trial.

"Path" connotes walking, moving, changing. That is half our life. "Lying down" connotes the other half of life: our being, our identity. God is the Creator, Designer, Knower, and Standard for both.

Both our acting and our being, both what we do and what we are, have "ways", that is, character, personality. Our life (each action) both causes and is caused by personality (being). The plot of a story is both shaped by and shapes characters, for what they do is determined by what they are and what they are is determined by what they do. God knows it all: the human subjects (the characters) and the natural objects (the setting, the universe) and the plot (the actions, the life). He both "compasses" and "encompasses" it all.

Sanity consists most essentially in affirming this fact (that God knows it all) and loving it. Insanity consists most essentially in denying this fact (by ignoring or denying Truth, whose name is God) or, even worse, by hating it (preferring darkness to light). That, in the last analysis, is what makes the difference between Heaven and Hell. God is unalterable light, and He shines everywhere. Those in Heaven are blessed and blissed by that light, that truth, that divine gaze, unalterably and forever. Those in Hell are tortured by it, by the very same fact, unalterably and forever.

> For there is not a word in my tongue, but, lo,
>   O LORD, thou knowest it altogether.

"A word in my tongue" is always the expression of "a thought in my mind and heart". We know other people only after we hear them, but God knows the mind and heart even before they are expressed, as Shakespeare knows what Hamlet will say before he says it and what

Hamlet will think before he thinks it, because he created and designed Hamlet. (This does not remove Hamlet's free will; in fact, it constitutes it, it creates it. It is Shakespeare's will that Hamlet be a free person, not an unfree thing like his sword or his castle.)

The only things that any of us can know "altogether", i.e., completely, with no mystery and no ambiguity, are probably numbers. God knows *everything* and everyone "altogether".

There is an even greater difference between our knowledge and God's: we know things because they are real; they are real because God knows them. (See the last paragraph on page 49 on this.)

> Thou hast beset me behind and before,
> and laid thine hand upon me.

We meet other creatures only in our present. (Our present includes our present memories of our past and our present anticipations, fears, and hopes for our future.) But we meet God also "behind and before". He comes to us from our past and even from our future. We meet Him coming to us out of our past and coming to us out of our future, since for Him the past (that is, what to us is the past) is not dead and the future (that is, what to us is the future) is not unborn. Both our past and our future are as real to Him as our present is to us. He is still there, in our past, and He is already there, in our future. Not only can we not escape Him in space, by flying to some remote place "in the uttermost parts of the sea", but we cannot escape Him in time, either, in past or present or future. His "is" includes "was" and "will be". Ours does not. Hamlet's present is encompassed and walled in by his past and future (indeed, that is part of his torment), but

Shakespeare's present "encompasses" all three dimensions of Hamlet's time since he designs and creates it.

This Shakespeare-and-Hamlet analogy for God-and-us is not "predestination". It is simply destination, design. For there is no "pre" in the Designer, only in the design. God does not look into the future as a fortune-teller looks into a crystal ball. God already is in the future, as He still is in the past.

(If you did not understand that, welcome to the human race. Augustine famously said, about time, that we understand it only when we are not asked about it.)

Since our imagination is limited to and dependent on our past experience, and since we have not yet experienced God's eternal life, we cannot *imagine* what that divine all-present and all-encompassing life is. We can only imagine what it is not. Therefore, our word for it is negative, not positive: "*e*-ternity" means "*not*-temporality". It does not mean merely unending time, which would be only more and more of the life we now have. It is a different kind of life. It is a life that is natural to God and supernatural to us, but God has deigned to allow us to know about it and to hope for it and actually to participate in it, to share it, to live it, with Him after death ends the old time, the time that was part of the universe that we will leave behind, which is the time that separates, the time of good-byes. Heaven's time will be the time that unites, the time of hellos.

It is God's power (symbolized by His "hand") as well as His knowledge that encompass us in a way that transcends the limitations of time. The Creator has total power over His creatures. If the Creator were limited by time as the creature is, His power would also be limited. He is not, and therefore it is not. Once again, this is something we cannot imagine because it is not in our experience.

The practical payoff for this theology of omnipotence is trust. We can have total trust only in an omnipotent being (there is only one!); we can have only partial trust in a being who has only superior, but limited power. Trust in anyone, human or divine, is limited by three things: that someone's power, knowledge, and benevolence. That "someone" might lack the power to help us even if he does not lack the wisdom or goodwill (think of a very wise and saintly human being); or he might lack the wisdom to know what is best for us even if he does not lack the power or the goodwill (think of a bumbling giant with great power and good intentions); or he might lack the goodwill to help us even if he does not lack the power or the knowledge (think of the Hindu Brahman, an all-knowing consciousness without a discriminating moral will, who does not say "Choose life" [Deut 30:19] but is equally in Vishnu the creator and Shiva the destroyer). But since God's power, knowledge, and benevolence are all unlimited, our trust in Him can and should also be unlimited. Thus Romans 8:28: this God, and only this God, makes all things work together for good for us who love and trust Him.

Our only reason for total trust is that we are under both the "hand" (omnipotence) and the mind (omniscience) of God and that that infinite power and wisdom are also infinite love and mercy. The first two truths (God's omnipotence and omniscience) are necessary and therefore provable by good philosophy and theology. The third truth (God's mercy, which goes beyond justice) is God's free choice and, therefore, can only be believed in and hoped for, not proved.

That is why religion goes beyond philosophy and philosophical theology, as faith goes beyond even the highest heights of reason. Reason climbs Everest, but faith grows wings and flies. Philosophical theology is a science ("the science of God"), and therefore it appeals only to reason, not to faith. It cannot know as much about God as religion can, for "religion" (from *religare*) literally means "binding (personal faith-) relationship". Theology explores the art, religion listens to the Artist.

(There is also a third enterprise, which is sort of half-way between a purely rational philosophical theology and the lived faith, hope, and love relationship that is religion, namely, revealed theology, which uses reason to under-stand and deduce from the divine revelation that is believed by faith and lived and experienced by hope and love.)

> Such knowledge is too wonderful for me;
> it is high, I cannot attain unto it.

If you did not understand the preceding points about time and eternity at all, that is O.K. You are sane and normal. If you did understand it a little, well, then, con-gratulations, but you are probably in trouble, for you are probably tempted to think that you comprehend it more than you do. No, you do not. No one does, certainly not this writer. Partial understanding, maybe; but compre-hension, adequate understanding—never. "Such knowl-edge is too wonderful for me" because it is "high", it is proper to God, not to man. Aquinas says that no man can understand everything about *anything*, not even one little flea.

So if you clearly and adequately understand nothing about God except the fact that you clearly and adequately understand nothing about Him, then good for you: that is the first and most important thing to understand. That is Lesson One, and David is here confessing that he has learned it. But if you think you clearly or adequately understand more than that, then shame on you. Your lessons two through two million are worth nothing if you forget Lesson One.

What good is it, then, for us to look up at this divine knowledge if it is unattainable? What good does it do us to look up at the mountain if we cannot climb it, at the eagle if we cannot fly, or at the stars if we cannot go there? What good is it for us to know there is a God?

What a stunningly stupid question! As Browning says, "a man's reach should exceed his grasp, or what's a heaven for?" To ask what good is our sight of the unreachable mountain, the eagle, or the stars is to ask why sight is better than blindness.

To ask that stunningly stupid question is to lack humility. Saint Bernard of Clairvaux, asked to name the four cardinal virtues, replied: "Humility, humility, humility, and humility." Humility is not skepticism. Skepticism is pride. Skepticism is an ism. In fact, it is a claim to certainty. It claims to be certain that we can never be certain. Humility is not an ism, it is a hope. What does it hope for? It hopes for divine grace to carry our souls beyond the stars that we see, through the angels that we do not see, and to live to see the face of the God, whose face no man can see and live (Ex 33:20).

> Whither shall I go from thy spirit?
> or whither shall I flee from thy presence?

It is even more obviously impossible to escape the Omnipresence in space than in time. For time includes minds and spirits as well as bodies, but space includes only bodies. We cannot have any image of God's temporal omnipresence, but we can form some images of his spatial omnipresence, if only inadequate ones. For instance, energy and activity are everywhere in the universe. They are inescapable, like light, like Truth.

To flee from a rabid dog is a reasonable thing. To flee from Truth is not. The Hound of Heaven is not a rabid dog. He is our healing Father. He is inescapable because He is Truth and Light; and darkness has absolutely no defense against light. That fact is either our supreme joy or our supreme terror.

David is here rejoicing in the fact that all his desperate, foolish attempts to escape God's presence are doomed to failure. That holy fact can be either denied or affirmed with the mind and either loved or hated with the heart. Thus there are only four possibilities in relation to this Primary Fact. It can be

(1) denied, with (deceptively) happy relief, or
(2) denied, with unhappy regret, or
(3) affirmed, with happy hope and joy, or
(4) affirmed, with unhappy terror.

The happy, comfortable atheist (like Sartre) embraces the first alternative.

The honest and therefore unhappy and uncomfortable atheist (like Camus) embraces the second.

The wise Jew, Christian, or Muslim affirms the third.

The Devil affirms the fourth.

> If I ascend up into heaven, thou art there:
> if I make my bed in hell, behold, thou art there.

The physical "heavens", full of lights, are a natural icon or holy symbol for the spiritual life of the Heaven of God; and the darkness of sleeping and dreaming ("my bed") is a natural symbol for the spiritual death that is Hell. But the word translated "hell" here does not mean what Jesus called "Gehenna", which was the garbage dump outside Jerusalem. Gehenna contained two things: (1) garbage, which used to be food, and (2) fire, which continually consumed it and never went out. Thus Hell contains (1) the spiritual garbage which used to be human souls and (2) unending and therefore hopeless destruction. But "hell" here translates, not Gehenna, but Sheol. Sheol means simply the grave, the state of being dead, which is darkness, for it is not known to the living.

Even in this Sheol, there are two persons we cannot escape: ourselves and God, both of whom are called "I", for each of us is the image of the Great "I AM." We cannot escape either "I" anywhere or anywhen, either in time or in eternity, for a single moment.

That is why suicide is always a mistake: because it seeks the impossible: to escape from either or both of those two inescapable persons. Suicide happens only when the relation between those two persons (self and God) is some kind of war rather than peace; and the warring soul seeks to escape the battle by escaping from either or both of those two persons, but it cannot. And therefore it cannot escape any of the pains or problems in the war from which the suicide so naturally desires to escape. For it does not realize that all our problems are ultimately rooted in our misrelation to the God who is the source of all joy, and not first of all in other people or the material world. As Thomas Merton says, "we are not at peace with others because we are not at peace with ourselves, and we are not at peace with ourselves because we are not at peace with God." (This does not mean that we can have no hope for suicides. We must, and therefore can, have hope for everyone.)

God is present to everything real. Both life and death are real. Therefore, God is present to both life and death.

Supernatural life (Heaven) and natural life (which is both
a living and a dying) and subnatural life (physical and temporal death, Sheol) and antinatural life (spiritual and eternal death, Hell, Gehenna) are all real; therefore, God is
present, in different ways, to all of them.

How is God present in Hell (Gehenna)? Is not Hell to
be forsaken of God? Yes, but forsakenness is a kind of
presence. If God were not real, no one could be deprived
of Him. No one is deprived of unicorns. Saints and mystics often say that God is present in Hell, too, but those in
Hell hate that Light and Truth and Righteousness, while
those in Heaven love them. The same reality—God, and
that which God essentially is—can be my food and your
poison, my bliss and your torture. Take two people to an
opera: for the first one, it is Heaven; for the second, it is
Hell. Now take them to a hard rock concert. For the first
one, it is Hell; for the second, it is Heaven.

> If I take the wings of the morning, and dwell in the
>   uttermost parts of the sea;
> Even there shall thy hand lead me, and thy right
>   hand shall hold me.

Changing our place, traveling through space (whether on
earth or beyond the earth) cannot escape God's "hand"
as it can escape a human hand (e.g., the hand of a tyrant),
because "He's got the whole world in His hands." His
hands are not in the world; the world is in His hands.
His hands made the world. We can neither hold Him nor
release Him; He holds us and never releases us.

"The wings of the morning" here might mean the wings
of a bird that flies only when morning comes. Or it might
mean the wings of the morning itself. Perhaps David here
imagines morning as a gigantic bird. We can stop ordinary

birds from flying to any particular place, but we cannot stop the morning coming to every place on earth. But even the morning is only a creature, and no creature can escape the Creator even if it rides on gigantic wings.

Imagine someone trying to escape the morning light by continually flying around the earth at the same rate as the morning (sunlight) comes. He can live in perpetual night. But even this does not keep out the light of God, as the next verse shows. As Augustine says, when we try to hide ourselves from God, we only hide God from ourselves, not ourselves from Him. When we run away from the sun, we run into our own shadow. Hell consists in the self finally disappearing into that shadow as into a Black Hole.

> If I say, Surely the darkness shall cover me,
> even the night shall be light about me.
> Yea, the darkness hideth not from thee; but the night
>   shineth as the day:
> the darkness and the light are both alike to thee.

God has night vision. He does not need light to see. We see only by light, whether physical light or mental light. "God is light, and in him is no darkness at all." Light comes *from* Him who said "Let there be light", and there was light.

Evil loves the darkness. That is why most crimes are committed at night, and why we hide our sins but not our virtues, and why all sins resist honesty, confession, and repentance as maggots, cockroaches, and rats resist light. That is also why honesty, humility, confession, and repentance are the surest barrier against sin, the most powerful antidote to sins. All sins are sins against the light.

When David says that "the darkness and the light are both alike to thee", he does not mean to equate God with "the Force" in *Star Wars*, which is half-darkness and half-light, half-evil and half-good. Darkness and light are not the same *morally* to God, but they are the same *intellectually* or *epistemically*; they are both equally *known*.

This verse also can be interpreted to imply that God fully understands all our human darkness: not only moral darkness, but also intellectual darkness, the severest mental retardation and brain damage, the darkest insanity that resists all the light of human reason. The world's best psychologists and psychiatrists often admit that they simply cannot get inside the minds of some of their "worst cases" because the darkness is too thick and deep. That is not the case with God. He is there, even in the darkest mind. He is in the deepest mine and the darkest mind.

And not only *minds* and *mines* but also *mine*—my mind, my mental mine, my darkness. For we all have some darkness within. When we meet a morally or intellectually insane person, we meet only a larger version of part of ourselves. The difference is only in quantity, not quality. We are not another species. They are our brothers and sisters. If we are to speak the truth, we must say "There but for the grace of God go I." When we see them, we are not looking out a window into something outside ourselves, but we are looking at something inside ourselves; we are looking into a mirror. Indeed, one of the reasons why God arranges for them to exist and to impinge on our lives is to show us ourselves. This is true of all "the handicapped", for we are all "the handicapped" in some way.

But God totally understands and totally loves all of His severely brain-damaged children.

> For thou hast possessed my reins:
> thou hast covered me in my mother's womb.

Here are two similar images for God's encompassing omniscience and omnipotence. First, since "reins" is an old word for kidneys, it means that God knows our most inward and invisible parts. Second, He "covers" us as a mother covers a sleeping baby. His knowledge totally encloses us, like the blanket that comes from our mother's love. He surrounds us, "covers us over". It is essentially the same image as "(en)compassing".

Neither relationship can be reversed. The kidney cannot know or possess the body; the body "knows" and "possesses" its kidneys. The baby cannot surround and cover the mother. The baby has no womb to contain the mother, but the mother has a womb to contain the baby. And even after birth, the mother continues to "enwomb" the baby with protection, love, food, and blankets. God mothers us as well as fathering us (Mt 23:37). Male and female are both "the image of God" (Gen 1:27).

Both images are humbling. (They are meant to be that, meant to shock and surprise our pride.) We are only kidneys. We are not adults, we are not even children; we are only babies, in fact, unborn babies, still in the womb that is this universe. When we die and leave the larger womb of the maternal, material universe, we will look back on that universe which we thought was so unimaginably vast as we now look back on our mother's womb: as a small, confining thing. When we were in our mother's womb, we thought *that* was enormous. In fact, it seemed like the totality of being.

Yet, although both images are humbling, they are also utterly comforting if we trust Him (and utterly terrifying if we do not). He is the perfect kidney surgeon. He is also the perfect mother. He is the shepherd; we are the sheep. He is the author; we are His characters. He is the Creator; we are His creatures. He is everything; we are almost nothing. When Lady Julian of Norwich was given a mystical vision by God, she saw a tiny hazelnut in His hand, and she asked, "What is that?"

God replied, "That is all things that are made." All the galaxies and all the angels, all the hundreds of billions of galaxies and billions of years, past and future, all things without exception are in that tiny hazelnut. "He's got the whole world in His hands."

> I will praise thee; for I am fearfully and wonderfully
>   made:
> marvellous are thy works; and that my soul knoweth
>   right well.

All God's works are marvelous and worthy of praise, but by far the greatest work is Man, who alone bears the very image of God.

If you want to see God Himself, look at His Son. For "he that hath seen me hath seen the Father." The Son is the total Mind, Manifestation, or Word of the Father; and the Spirit is Their total love. The Son (*His* Son) is truth (logos, mind, intelligence), and the Spirit (*Their* Spirit) is love (the love between the Father and the Son). In God, truth and love are so real that they are not principles, abstractions, ideals, or ideas, they are Persons.

The ultimate reason why we are "fearfully and wonderfully made" is because we are made in His Trinitarian image; we, like God, are Mind and Will; we can know truth and love goodness. Nothing is more marvelous than that, because nothing is more marvelous than God, and God is that. When He created us in His own image, Chesterton says, "God broke His own law, and made a graven image of Himself."

This is so "wonderful" that it is "fearful". This is so "marvelous" that it is almost unendurable, like a beauty so perfect that it makes you fear you will just fade away and disappear in its presence like fog at sunrise. That is how Dante felt when he saw Beatrice in Heaven, in *The Divine Comedy*.

The only possible reaction to this marvel is praise. Not proper, controlled praise, but "fanatical" praise, crazy wild praise, praise without borders, without proofs or justifications, praise beyond all thoughts and feelings. And the knowledge of this beauty is not some secret, esoteric knowledge reserved for monks in mystical experience. It is what the practical King David confesses "that my soul knoweth right well". And so do you. So you have absolutely no excuse, in time or eternity, for not laying down this book for a minute, turning your soul inside out, and spilling out your deepest guts to God in praise. Whoop! If there are other people near you, excuse yourself and go to the bathroom, thank Him for its privacy, and praise Him there. We can turn a bathroom into a cathedral. (We can also turn a cathedral into a bathroom.) If there is no one near you, go wild for God right here and now. Because God went wild for you. Twice, in fact: when He created you and when He redeemed you; when He gave you life on earth in your mother's womb (one of the two holiest places on earth) and when He gave you life in Heaven by giving you His own life, on the Cross and in the Eucharist, which is the other holiest place. (That is why contraception is sacrilegious: it is as Christophobic as fear of the Eucharist.)

> My substance was not hid from thee, when I was
> made in secret,
> and curiously wrought in the lowest parts of the
> earth.

"My substance" does not mean "my chemicals"; it means "my essential nature, my self, my *me*". Even when I was a one-celled zygote. *You* were once a zygote, just as you were once an infant. There is only one you, no matter how much you change.

"The lowest parts of the earth" do not mean the Dead Sea, the iron core at the planet's center, or the deepest coal mine (your mother did not conceive you there), but in the darkest, most hidden place, the womb. It is the light that is "the lowest" there, not the altitude.

Perhaps we could add a second interpretation to "the lowest parts of the earth". They could mean the earliest, most primitive parts of our story, i.e., all the matter and energy in the universe at its beginning, when it was all condensed into an infinitesimally tiny dot immediately after the act of creation, which our science has discovered and called "the Big Bang". God had you in mind when He banged out the Big Bang. That is why He did it. Why else do you think He did it? For gases and galaxies? No, they are just the raw material. It was for you that He created the universe. He took a long time (over thirteen billion years) to take a very little bit of that matter and to form it into you. But you were His goal from the beginning.

We are all made of "star stuff". It took 13.8 billion years for the womb of the universe to produce your mother and her womb. Then it took nine months for her to grow you in that garden. And it probably will take seventy or eighty or ninety years or so to get you through this second womb that we call the world, or the universe, to get you through the birth canal of death and into the larger world of Heaven. Your life is a story with a plot, and you are the protagonist, and the universe is only the setting.

> Thine eyes did see my substance, yet being unperfect;
> and in thy book all my members were written,
> which in continuance were fashioned, when as yet
>   there was none of them.

The old-fashioned language can be charming rather than puzzling and bothersome if only we understand it. "My substance" means "my essential being". "Unperfect" means, not just "less than perfectly good", but "not yet fully made". The English word "perfect" comes from the two Latin words for "through" and "made", "per-factum". We are made through a process, like a cake that is baked. But God knew us from the beginning, when our substance, our essence, was not yet in the world but only in His planning mind. In this divine mind, which David symbolizes as a book (think of a cookbook for baking the cake), all my "members", i.e., organs and body parts, were "written", i.e., planned, like ingredients in the recipe. Even before any of them existed, all were known. God knew you and loved you into existence when you were conceived in your mother's womb, but He has known and loved you from before you were conceived. In fact, He has known you and loved you for 13.8 billion years. For, as we have seen when we explored the last verse of Psalm 1, His knowledge does not conform to a reality outside of Him; rather, it makes it; and all reality other than He conforms to His knowing, not vice versa. His knowledge, therefore, does not await reality, as ours does (we have to wait until we really *are* fifty to know we are fifty); reality awaits His knowledge, His creative act of knowing it into existence. He is an artist, not a scientist.

Bottom line: God not only knows everything that is, was, or will be, but He knows it before it exists. He thinks the universe and us into existence. That is the ultimate reason why He is inescapable.

> How precious also are thy thoughts unto me, O God!
> how great is the sum of them!
> If I should count them, they are more in number than
> the sand:
> when I awake, I am still with thee.

To the wicked, who seek darkness, these thoughts—God's thoughts, which determine us and cause us and create us— are not at all "precious" but threatening to their freedom. That is the deepest motive behind atheism. We see it in the well-known atheists like Sartre and Nietzsche, who freely admit it. That is always an ultimate option, the No. The other is the Yes, the "hurrah", the praise, the judgment of "precious". For Sartre, freedom is always a No, and the Yes to the Other is always a compromise to freedom. Nietzsche confesses that he could not live in a world in which God saw his dark side.

What is common to both opposite responses to God, the No and the Yes, is the size of God, so to speak. Any God worthy of the name must make a total difference to the totality of things. For God is not just very great, He is infinitely great.

Something physical that is almost immeasurably large is an image of the literal infinity of God: the sea, all the grains of sand on all the beaches in the world, all the stars in the sky, or the universe itself. At these one feels either awe and wonder and humility and gratitude, which leads to worship, or else terror or envy, which leads to resentment and rebellion against Being itself, against Truth, against the Way Things Are. Atheists believe they would feel negated and flattened and destroyed and terrified by this immense weight. But theists feel affirmed and enlarged and made real and blessed and blissed by it. They pray, in the "Gloria", "We give thanks to Thee for Thy great glory", thanking God, not just for His gifts, but for the sheer fact of being Himself.

Why do they feel this way? Because theists have faith and trust that behind this infinite and inescapable knowledge and power is love. Atheists do not. That is the difference faith makes. That is why the difference faith makes is the difference between Heaven and Hell. It is not that Heaven is a reward God decides to give for faith and Hell a punishment for faithlessness. Rewards and punishments can be revoked; this is simply The Way Things Necessarily Are.

"When I awake, I am still with thee." What does this mean? It means that death is a kind of awakening from sleep, from the "shadowlands", from this life in which we see God only "through a glass darkly" and, therefore, need to add faith to that sight. It means that in this life we try to count what we cannot count, namely, the grains of sand and the thoughts of God; and when we awake from this life, we awake from that counting, from the world in which mathematics is the language of the universe. When we awake from death, we will be in a very different life and a very different universe, but not with a different God. The God who will be with us (in an incomprehensibly more intimate and perfect way) in the next life is the same God who is with us now, just as truly "with" us, just as truly present, though we see Him only by faith. And He is just as truly our greatest joy, in fact, our only joy, in the last analysis, now, in this life, as He will be in Heaven. For there is no other joy. That is The Way Things Are, that is The Primary Fact, that is The Unchangeable and Inescapable Truth. To those who hate and resent it as a limit and an affront to their so-called freedom, that truth is Hell. To those who love it, it is Heaven.

> Surely thou wilt slay the wicked, O God:
> depart from me therefore, ye bloody men.

Why did God deliberately allow David to add this hatefully ugly postscript to this lovingly beautiful psalm? For our instruction. There are three parts to this psalm. All

that went before this verse was part one. The next three
verses, beginning here, David's plea to God to please kill
his enemies, is part two. The last two verses of the psalm
are part three. In part one, David reveals his profound
holiness and his wisdom. In part two, David reveals his
profound unholiness and foolishness. In part three, David
reveals that his holiness and wisdom triumph even over his
shocking unholiness and foolishness. (You might want to
look briefly at those last two verses now.)

Part two, which starts here, is there for two reasons:
first, so that we can see the unholiness and ugliness of our
own souls reflected in the bright mirror of this great saint;
and second, so that we may be even more honest than we
were in part one, by allowing God's light to expose and
purge even the sins that we confuse with virtues, as David
does in part two. Part two is there for the sake of part
three, where he questions his part two, for part three is the
part we need the most.

Why did David express this shocking hatred immediately
after expressing His profound love of God? We must understand that in David's mind, the two are not in contrast at
all. For he knows one-half of the truth without the other:
he knows that the wicked—the truly, down-to-the-core,
rotten-at-the-core, Hell-bound wicked—are indeed to God
what darkness is to light or what cancer is to living cells; and
the more you love the light, the more you hate the darkness. What he does not know is the depth of God's love and
grace and mercy and forgiveness. But what he does know,
he knows truly and profoundly. For he is flawed, but he is
wise and holy. We are not wise enough, or holy enough,
to be as shockingly unholy as David. We lukewarm, polite
moderns do not hate the Hellish darkness as passionately as
David does because we do not love the Heavenly light
as much as he does.

It is true that hating the darkness allows the darkness
to enter our soul because hate *is* that darkness. But let us
not be self-righteous snobs. It is true that David here fails
to make the crucial distinction between sinners and sins
("love the sinner, hate the sin"), for he is a "primitive",
a simple child, not a modern, sophisticated adult. Only
Jesus Christ was ever both of those things fully at the same
time: "primitive" and "sophisticated". (Saint Paul and
Saint Augustine came close.) Only God can perfectly reconcile justice and mercy, and he does it by having justice
simultaneously come down from Heaven and arise from
earth when He incarnates and sacrifices Himself for us on
Calvary (Ps 85:10–11; please read those two verses now).

David then speaks to God as if he had to remind Him of
how wicked the wicked are:

> For they speak against thee wickedly,
> and thine enemies take thy name in vain.

David here justifies his hate by pointing out to God a fact,
as if He did not know it. How many of our prayers seek
to inform the Omniscience of what He seems to ignore
and to redirect His Providence? They often imply a sentence beginning with "If I were You, I would...." That
sentence is always one of the stupidest sentences we can
ever say.

> Do not I hate them, O LORD, that hate thee?
> and am not I grieved with those that rise up against thee?
> I hate them with perfect hatred:
> I count them mine enemies.

David is bragging about his sin as if it were his virtue.
"Put your Good Housekeeping Seal of Approval on me,

O God. Look how good I am! Look how much I hate
the wicked! Look how perfect my hate is! I am totally
and passionately on your side, God, in your war against
wickedness."

Good for David for being totally and passionately on
God's side, but God's side is no more the hatred of the
wicked than it is the love of wickedness. David could not
have understood that last sentence. He sees the First Virtue, the root of all virtue, which is justice and righteousness, so clearly that he cannot see the Second Virtue, the
fruit of all virtue, which is love and mercy. We have to
sympathize with David here. After all, there are only two
sides to the war that this life is: there is good, and there is
evil; there is light, and there is darkness. David cannot see
any third possibility here at all. And what he sees is true:
that "God is light, and in him is no darkness at all"; that
God is just and loves justice and hates wickedness. But He
does not hate the wicked. He loves them. That is why
He died for them, for His enemies. Who are His enemies?
"We have met the enemy and he is us."

David does a bad thing for a good reason: he hates the
wicked because he hates wickedness. He does not realize
that this hate *is* wickedness as well as righteousness. Hatred
of wickedness is righteousness and justice; hatred of the
wicked is wickedness and mercilessness. It is very hard,
perhaps impossible, for us to be totally, passionately just
and totally, passionately merciful. But "the things which
are impossible with men are possible with God."

Please do not feel superior to David because you understand the distinction between sins and sinners or because
you value love and mercy more than David does. His love
of God, as far as he imperfectly but truly knows Him, is
probably light-years ahead of yours. Please do not think
that your modern, sophisticated, civilized "tolerance" and

"compassion" to sinners is free from the same confusion you find in David's soul. David failed to see how much we must love sinners; we fail to see how much we should hate sins. David let his knowledge of justice and truth eclipse his knowledge of love, and this sometimes (for instance, here) turned his justice into a hard, even hating thing. But we make a similar mistake: we let our knowledge of love eclipse our knowledge of justice and truth, and this turns our love into a soft, weak, *comfortable* thing. We need to remind ourselves of Dostoyevsky's great truth that "love in action is a harsh and dreadful thing compared with love in dreams."

David thinks he is hating God's enemies with "perfect hatred", but he is mistaken. There is, indeed, such a thing as a perfect hatred, but he does not have it. God has it. Perfect hatred is the hatred of sins (and not of sinners) that is motivated purely by one thing: the love of sinners (and not of sins). See how hard it is for even a great saint to do that! Thank God God can do it! We would have no hope if He could not.

> Search me, O God, and know my heart:
> try me, and know my thoughts:
> And see if there be any wicked way in me,
> and lead me in the way everlasting.

This, which I have called part three of the psalm, is a triumphant return to total honesty and openness and humility, to the will to total nakedness before God and an implicit faith and trust in Him rather than a faith and trust in his own righteousness and his own wisdom that he had expressed in the previous few verses (part two). What David here understands is what Kierkegaard calls "the edification in the thought that over against God we are always in the wrong".

We are not always "over against God", but when we are, we are always in the wrong. How horrible it would be if we were not! That would be like waking up to find that the sun is a Black Hole, source of darkness and destruction rather than light and life.

This conversion from part two to part three is possible only on the basis of trust in God's goodness rather than our own. If we are wise enough not to trust ourselves, we can only fall helplessly at the feet of God. If we are fool-ish enough not to trust God, we will fall into the terrible trap of trusting ourselves. And those who trust in them-selves the most are in padded cells. "There goes a man who believes in himself." That is what they say when they welcome you to Hell.

David *wants* to be searched and known, tried and cor-rected by God. Does he not know that this is inevitably painful? That "our God is a consuming fire"? Or is he a fool who thinks he can just ooze comfortably into God like honey into tea? No, he may be a primitive fool who thinks, for a passing moment, that he is righteous in hating the wicked, but he is not a modern fool who thinks that the passage from wickedness to righteousness is easy. He knows it involves Purgatory. He knows this from his own experi-ence (see Ps 51). But he *wants* this Purgatory, as do the souls who are in it.

David is certain of God and uncertain of his own heart. That is why he asks God to judge his heart. Although he does not see any wickedness in his own heart (and there-fore he does not confess and repent of his previous hatred of his enemies), he no longer stands on and pleads his own righteousness, as he did in the preceding verses. That uncertainty about self is not a recipe for worry but one for joy, both in this life and in the next, even in Purgatory. Being uncertain of God and certain of yourself is a recipe for misery. Resting on our own righteousness is resting on the stuff we have in us when we sit on our great white throne of the toilet. David's trust now is in God's mercy, not His justice; he trusts that even if "there be a wicked way in me", God will lead him "in the way everlasting". (See how Psalm 1 is presupposed in all the psalms.)

Is God's mercy based on His ignoring the ugly truth that is brought to light by the searing light of His omniscience? Impossible. Or do God's justice and truth censor and limit and block His mercy, forgiveness, and love? Impossible. In God, justice and mercy, righteousness and forgiveness, light and life, truth and love, are *one thing*, and neither is compromised.

But in order to receive that one thing, which God has and is, we need to have the one thing that David has, which also has many names: faith, hope, love, trust, humility, honesty, openness, vulnerability, surrender, repentance, conversion.

Note that what we receive when we receive God's salvation is that unity of truth and love, of justice and mercy, that God Himself is. And therefore, what we receive is sanctification as well as justification. Salvation does not mean merely justification by His mercy and love and forgiveness but also sanctification by His truth and righteousness.

If we sincerely pray this prayer of David's, if we really want what we say we want in this prayer, we will certainly get it. "Blessed are they which do hunger and thirst after righteousness: for they shall be filled."

God is just one thing, though we see it and call it by two different names. One name is justice and righteousness and truth. The other name is mercy and forgiveness and love. In God, there is no distinction between these two things. In Eden, there was no distinction between these two things for us, either; and in Heaven there will again be no distinction between these two things for us, when Truth and Justice will not threaten us and demand repentance, as they do now. In all three places (Eden, earth now, and Heaven), our prayer "God, give me Your love" means "God, give me Heaven." But in the middle place, where we are now, in the "middle-earth" that is "East of Eden" and West of Heaven, "God, give me justice" means "God, give me damnation." David knows this well enough, inchoately, in the depths of his heart, to make him question his prayer to God for justice, to hedge his bets.

The answer to the question "What must I do to be saved?" is a single word; it is saying Yes with the whole heart and soul to God. There are many words for the many aspects of this Yes: faith, hope, love, trust, honesty, openness, surrender, submission, obedience. But this Yes is one thing. The plethora of words, necessary as they are, often mask it more than they reveal it. It is not too difficult or complex or mysterious for words; it is too simple for words. To learn it, look at that baby's face looking up into Mama's face. That is life's most advanced lesson. That is why God invented babies: to be our teachers.

Psalm 103

"Bless the LORD, O my soul"

This was my father's favorite psalm. I think there must be spiritual heredity as well as biological, because his love of it infected me, whether by heredity or by environment (example) or both. He asked me to read it to him when he knew he was dying. (For everything in this world, death-beds are the supreme test of values.) It broke his heart with happiness. And mine.

This is the psalm of a happy man. He is happy because he is grateful. That, in one word, is the key to happiness: gratitude. That is also the key to wisdom.

> Bless the LORD, O my soul,
> and all that is within me, bless his holy name.

How can we "bless the Lord"? God gives blessings to us, but how can we give blessings to Him? How can we add to infinity?

The answer is that "to bless" can mean two different things. It can mean to give someone something needed, to improve him, to make him happier. But no one can improve God or His infinite joy. The only way we can give anything to God is to give Him the two things that are the first two purposes of prayer: praise and adoration, and gratitude and thanksgiving. But this does not add to

God, only to us. We give it, not because God needs it, but because He deserves it. This is not to add anything to God but to add wisdom and happiness to us and to add to the unending cosmic chorus of praise from the angels and from every other creature in the universe, which is the very last thing said by the very last psalm: "Let every thing that hath breath praise the LORD!" (Ps 150:6). And it is also to shed God's glory among men and, thus, to improve other men, to invite them into the song, to make them wise and happy. Blessing is a three-way conversation. It improves both the human blessers and the human hearers, but not the divine Blessed One.

But it is also true that we *can* increase God's happiness by loving and praising and blessing Him. Because God the Son is still fully human as well as fully divine; because Christ's Ascension was not the undoing of His Incarnation; because the human nature of the second Divine Person of the Trinity is eternally united to His divine nature in what theologians call "the hypostatic union"; we can, indeed, increase God's happiness. For we can increase His human happiness by accepting His love. He loves us, and love thirsts for love. Read Mother Teresa's famous prayer meditation on those words from the Cross, "I thirst." (Google it.) Her whole vocation was motivated by that thirst.

David commands his soul to "bless the LORD." How can one command himself? What powers of the soul does David command to praise God? And with what powers of his soul is he commanding them? Are not the commanding officer and the commanded soldier here the same person? David is not two persons, but one. The answer is that he is commanding all of his powers with all of his powers: mind, memory, imagination, hope, love, trust, faith, desire, feelings, and, above all, will, for "to bless" is here *commanded* and, thus, willed. The will is the soul's captain.

But if all those things are included in what is commanded to the commandee, what is left in the commander? That is a mystery, and the only answer is the one Augustine gives in his *Confessions* when, in commanding his soul to give itself wholly to God, he wonders why, although the body obeys the soul, the soul does not obey itself. Body is not soul, and soul is not body, yet the gap between the two is instantly overcome every time our soul commands our body to act and it obeys—in eating, running, looking, lifting a hand. In stark contrast, although soul is soul—there is no gap—yet the soul does not obey itself. The body obeys the soul as if the two were one thing, but the soul disobeys itself as if the one soul were two things. Augustine is there wrestling with the same mystery with which Saint Paul wrestles in Romans 7:15 when he confesses that "what I would do, that do I not, but what I hate, that I do." "For what [good] I would [want, will], I do not; but what [evil] I hate, that I do" (v. 19). It is with the will that I will to do both the good and the evil; it is with the will that I both will to do the good and will not to do it. My will is divided. That is Augustine's discovery. If it were not divided, it would not have to command itself, and there would be no gap, no difference, between the willing and the doing.

Life is spiritual warfare, and the enemy is within, not without. We try to run from this fact: Adam blamed Eve, and Eve blamed the devil; but God did not accept either excuse. If we blame Adam, it is not a good bet that He will agree with us, either. God does not excuse, He forgives. If we do not know the difference between those two things, we probably misunderstand both. Excusing is very easy and cheap; forgiving is very hard and costly. We are the Church of the costly Cross, not the Church of Cheap Grace.

> Who forgiveth all thine iniquities;
> who healeth all thy diseases;

Iniquity is to the soul what disease is to the body. The body is the image of the soul. The best answer to the question "What does a human soul look like?" is Wittgenstein's answer: that it looks like a human body. That is why we see spiritual happiness in a physical smile and why "the eyes are the windows of the soul." It is almost a kind of magic. It is sacramental.

As health is the unity of the organs and systems, disease is their dis-unity and, therefore, their dis-ease, their war instead of their peace. Similarly, as holiness is the wholeness of the soul, sin is its division. (1) The appetites war against each other like wild animals. (2) The appetites war against the will, which commands them so weakly. We all know how hard it is to overcome lust and greed by self-control and to master our fears by courage. (3) The will wars against the rule of reason: we are "willful" like spoiled brats. (4) The will also commands the reason to rationalize and excuse its evil. (5) But since we also still will the good, the evil will also wills against itself, as explained above, as discovered by Saint Augustine in the *Confessions* and by Saint Paul in Romans 7. (6) The reason also turns away from God; it does not see and cannot endure the Beatific Vision. The whole soul is out of whack within itself because it is out of whack with God.

The principle of causality dictates that we cannot *give* ourselves any perfection that we do not *have*. If we are divided and not one, we cannot give ourselves oneness. Only the One who is one can give oneness to our divided souls. And when He does, He does not merely *forgive* but also *heals*. He does to our souls what medicine, diet, and exercise do to our body: He gives us wholeness. But He operates in cooperation with our free will, not by force or

violence, against our will, or magically, without it. He also
does it gradually rather than instantly because grace deals
with nature according to its nature, and our nature is to be
creatures of time.

The distinction we most need to be clear about here is
not the distinction between body and soul (we are probably *too* clear about that, seeing the body as a soulless
machine and the soul as a bodiless ghost) but the distinction between justification and sanctification, between forgiving and healing. Forgiving (justification) is His work.
He finished it Himself on the Cross, when He said, "It
is finished" (Jn 19:30). All we have to do, all we *can* do, is
to accept it by honest confession, sincere repentance, and
trusting faith. But healing (sanctification) is a cooperative
work. How well it "takes", and how quickly, is at least
partly up to us. Yet it is God who initiates it. We cannot
sanctify ourselves. The unholy cannot make itself holy.
We cannot pull ourselves up by our own bootstraps. We
can stop it by ourselves, but we cannot start it by ourselves. We are like faucet handles: God provides the
water, but we turn the handle to let it through—or not.
We choose to be either "on" (to one degree or another)
or "off".

And He gives us His water only if we want it and hunger after it. He provides the food, but we provide the hunger. "Blessed are they which do hunger and thirst after
righteousness: *for they shall be filled.*" It is a divine promise.
If we cannot trust God to keep His solemn promises, we
cannot trust anyone or anything. And then our life gradually falls apart. It is truly "God or nothing", as Cardinal
Sarah's great title puts it.

> Who redeemeth thy life from destruction;
> who crowneth thee with lovingkindness and tender
>   mercies;

Destruction is the opposite of construction, as disease is the opposite of ease. He does not prevent the destruction that sin creates in us, as He did for the Blessed Virgin Mary in her Immaculate Conception. But He redeems (literally, "buys back") us out of our self-imposed slavery by "ransoming" the slaves with a price: His own life's blood. We had the free will to choose to sell ourselves into slavery; but once we did, we lost the freedom to choose the opposite. We are now slaves to sin, sinaholics, addicts. A drug addict once had the freedom to choose not to become an addict, but once he choses addiction, he no longer has the same freedom to choose not to be an addict. (Addiction means precisely the opposite of freedom.) We forged the chains of our bondage with the strength of our freedom, but we cannot free ourselves because we gave away that strength. We are slaves to Satan, and only One is stronger than Satan. We have absolutely no other hope than Him. Without Him, our whole soul, our whole life, in time and in eternity, will be destroyed forever. Our relation to Him, i.e., our "religion", is not a part of our life; it is the key to our entire life. It is not one of our organs; it is our umbilical cord.

What could motivate God to redeem us at such a terrible price? Only a terribly loving kindness and a terribly tender mercy—a love so terrible that even the most brilliant intellect ever created, that of our supernatural enemy, could not foresee it or block it. Nothing can block it. The devil is a shark, but God is a tsunami.

Compassion, lovingkindness, and tender mercy motivated Him. With us, these things are emotions. They are closely related to but distinct from the essential and unchangeable core nature of love, which is goodwill; but they are emotions, waves on the sea that rise and fall. They are distinctively human emotions (animals do not have them), and they are precious, moral, and spiritual and, therefore, at least partly free: we can choose to suppress them or encourage them. Therefore, they are virtues, and we are responsible for them. Their lack is a moral fault. But still, they are passions, feelings, which rise and fall like the tides or the winds. They come in waves, like all forms of physical energy (though they are not physical but spiritual). But with God, they are aspects of His unchanging and unchangeable essence. They do not rise and fall. His love is just one thing and is not divided into parts, one part being the essence, which is an act of will, and other parts being properties that are passions of the heart, which rise and fall, as it is with us. The tenderness and kindness and mercy that to us are changing *manifestations* of love are for God aspects of its unchanging essence. God does not lack the virtues that to us are changing manifestations of love, but in Him they are not changing manifestations but unchanging, unchangeable, eternal, and essential aspects of His love, which is His essence. He does not lack these emotions; what He lacks is their passivity and their intermittent character and their changeability, and also the gap between the will and the emotions. Both the goods of the will and the goods of the emotions exist in God, but in God they are not different, as they are in us. Tender mercy and lovingkindness are as eternal and essential to Him as justice and goodwill.

Why, then, does it seem as if God is more merciful to us on one day than on another? Because our needs change, and our capacity to receive His graces changes; that is why it seems to us as if He Himself changes when He gives us more mercies one day than another. It is projection; we are projecting onto Him the limitation that time causes in us, like yodelers in a canyon hearing their own voices echoing back to them from the rocks.

But He does not hold anything back that we can take. As Mother Teresa loved to say, God cannot be outdone in generosity. He does not merely dole out these things like pennies to a beggar; as the psalm says, He "crowns" us with them. He makes us kings and queens. He shares His rule, His power, with us. Only a king can do this. And He does it. As Saint Francis of Assisi said, in the *Fioretti*, "Which, thinkest thou, is the readier, our Lord God to give us his grace, or we to receive it?"

> Who satisfieth thy mouth with good things;
> so that thy youth is renewed like the eagle's.

David is thinking of literal food in a literal mouth, but this is also a symbol of spiritual food that satisfies the desires of our heart, which is our spiritual mouth. (That is why Christ puts His own Body and Blood into our mouths.)

Our thoughts about material things are symbols of material things, but those material things, in turn, are symbols of spiritual things, as the body is a sign or symbol of the soul, and not vice versa. The food we eat is a symbol of spiritual food, and not vice versa, as Jesus pointed out to his disciples. They were in Samaria during the heat of the day and had just brought back some food from the town, and they wondered why Jesus was not eating it. Jesus said, "I have meat [food] to eat that you know not of" (Jn 4:32). They thought it was physical food, for they said, "Hath any man brought him aught to eat?" When he explained that his "meat" (food) was to do the will of the Father, they were disappointed because he was tired and hungry and they had hoped he had eaten "real" food. But that *is* "real" food. Doing God's will, the essence of sanctity, is the food, the life, of our souls. The food we eat is the symbol. It is material food, not spiritual food, that is only a symbol, because bodies are the symbols of souls, not souls of bodies. Similarly, Saint Paul sees human biological fatherhood as the symbol and sees the Fatherhood of God the literal meaning of fatherhood when he says "I bow my knees unto the Father of our Lord Jesus Christ, of whom the whole family in heaven and earth is named" (Eph 3:14–15).

"Open thy mouth wide, and I will fill it" (Ps 81:10), says our Father to His babies (us) in their (our) high chairs. It is what the mother bird says to her baby birds in their nest. We are *promised* the thing we pray for when we pray "give us this day our daily bread." We are not promised earthly bread (some do, tragically, starve), but we are promised what is infinitely more needful, the Heavenly bread that is the "one thing needful" (Lk 10:42). No one ever need starve spiritually. The solemn divine promise "Seek, and ye shall find; ... he that seeketh, findeth" (Mt 7:7–8) applies, not to any of the countless things of this world, but only to the one thing that counts: God, who is the "one thing needful".

How can our youth "be renewed like the eagle's"? The ancients seem to have believed that old eagles could become young again. God used this myth, this biological error, to teach a profound truth: that all the good things of our youth, of our past, that seem to be lost forever because of time, are not lost forever but stored in Him and restored to us in eternity, which somehow includes all time rather than excluding it.

Perhaps this is done by an intensification of memory, so that in Heaven's present, we can somehow actually re-live the past. (Something like that seems to happen to many people at the moment of death.) We do not know *how* God does this. The "how" is only speculation: we understand God's "spiritual technology" about as well as cavemen understood spaceships. But there is a fact here. What fact? That in the resurrection and in the resurrection body, we will get back, in some transformed but true form, all the true goods and glories of youth that we thought time stole from us forever. God, not time, is the master of forever.

> The LORD executeth righteousness and judgment for
>   all that are oppressed.
> He made known his ways unto Moses,
> his acts unto the children of Israel.

God is the executive as well as the legislative and the judicial branches of the government of the universe. As excutive He executes justice; that is, He makes justice to prevail with His providential power. This is the justice He defines with His infallible mind ("judgment"), and this is His judicial function. This is also the justice that He legislates as "righteousness", and this is His legislative function. He joins power to execute justice, wisdom to define justice, and goodness to legislate justice; omnipotence, omniscience, and omnibenevolence. That is why "all things work together for good to them that love God" (Rom 8:28). This amazing and almost unbelievable good news follows logically from the three most necessary and nonnegotiable divine attributes of infinite power, infinite wisdom, and infinite goodness (goodwill, love).

How does God "execute righteousness and judgment"? In two ways: by justice and by mercy.

First, justice. We need justice because we are oppressed by injustice from ourselves (we oppress ourselves) as well as from others. "All that are oppressed" does not mean only one class of people, as in Marxism, but all, for all are sinners, and sin is injustice to the sinner, to others, and to God. But God's justice infallibly triumphs over man's injustice in the end. No one gets away with anything, in the long run, thank God!

The Law that He "made known to Moses", and through Moses to Israel, He also made known through Israel to the world, especially to Christians and Muslims, both of whom learned who the true God was and what His perfect Law was from the Jews, our common "fathers in the Faith", His collective prophet to the world.

It worked. In Abraham's time, no one knew the true God. Abraham was the first, the first Jew. In Moses' time, before the Ten Commandments, no one knew God's will or God's character very clearly. Paganism was largely darkness and confusion. Now half the world knows this perfect Law, for half the world now knows and worships the one true God, the God of Abraham, Israel, and Moses. Why? Because they were converted by Christian missionaries and by Christian heretics (Muslims, theologically defined, are Christian heretics, Nestorians).

Muslims do not know Christ as the Way to God (they reduce Him to a human prophet), but they do know the one true God because they learned of Him from the very same people we Christians did: from the Jews (both directly and through Christians). That is why the ninety-nine names of Allah in the Koran are all in the Bible, too. Muslims do not know God as intimately as Christians do, but the God they know in their pious but primitive, faithful but fearful way is the same God known by Adam, Noah, Abraham, Moses, David, the prophets, and Jesus.

Of course, David could not have known this future. All he knew about God's dealings with mankind was that in the past "he made known his ways unto Moses, his acts [miracles] unto the children of Israel." This was a "narrow" strategy on God's part, like laser light: focusing His revelation on one people and, within them, for a time, on Moses alone. No one else ever saw God face to face in this world and lived. His focus on Israel did not contradict but fulfilled His love for all peoples, as His focus on Moses did not contradict but fulfilled his love for all Jews. Moses was to the Jews what the Jews were to the world. Both choices worked: the result of this narrow strategy was the broadest miracle in history: the conversion of half the world to a knowledge of the true God.

Second, God executes righteousness by mercy, by giving us, through Christ's atonement for our sins, the righteousness we lack. God reconciled the demands of justice and mercy in Christ: Christ got the justice, and we got the mercy.

No one knows how much history is left, before The End, but I would not be surprised if the next two hundred years saw the conversion of billions more in a great expansion. Nor would I be surprised by a great contraction, if the next two hundred years saw a great apostasy. That seems to be closer to the scenario given in Revelation. The only thing we can know about the future is that we cannot know it. We never surprise Him, but God always surprises us.

> The LORD is merciful and gracious,
> slow to anger, and plenteous in mercy.

Among the ancient pagans, a few wise and holy sages knew that God was one. A few even knew that He was righteous and just. But why would the Lord of the universe show not just justice but mercy and grace to rebellious, sinful man? How could Perfect Justice be merciful? Among us, it is impossible. Either we give out the punishments that justice demands for evil, in which case we are just but not merciful; or else we do not, in which case we are merciful but not just. Without divine revelation, no man ever dreamed that the God of infinite power, knowledge, and justice could also be a God of infinite mercy and love. That was almost as big a surprise as the Incarnation.

And that is what the Bible is all about: God's self-revelation. The Bible does not ever bother to try to prove that God exists. Only "the fool" has "said in his heart, There is no God" (Ps 14:1), and he does that because he is not just an intellectual fool but also a moral fool: because he does not *want* there to exist a God who knows our sins and judges them. The Bible reveals to us, not the non-startling wisdom that God has existence, life, power, wisdom, and justice, all of which can be proved by good rational philosophy, but the startling and unpredictable "good news" that this God freely chooses to have mercy and love and tenderness and forgiveness toward His rebellious children.

Yet we have so domesticated what is startling that we now take for granted that God is loving and merciful, and we have so questioned what is necessary and obvious that we doubt that God is just, or even that He exists. (What is an atheist pop psychologist? Someone who believes that God does not exist and He loves you just as you are.) We believe the unbelievable, but we doubt the indubitable.

> He will not always chide:
> neither will he keep his anger for ever.

"Chiding" is an act of loving warning toward sinners and an act of hate and condemnation toward sins. Prophets chide. It is an act of charity. It is like Purgatory. What, then, does it mean that God will not always chide? It means that there are two places where God does not chide.

The two places are Heaven and Hell. There is no chiding in Heaven because there is no sin in Heaven. There is no chiding in Hell because there is nothing but sin in Hell, no alternative, no hope, and no more free choice to repent. You do not waste time shouting chidings and warnings at someone who has already jumped off the bridge, only at someone who is about to.

God's anger does not last forever because its object, sin, does not last forever. This is good news to the good and bad news to the bad. It is good news to the good because it means that at some time in your future God will find in you nothing to be angry about: you are destined to be a saint. It is bad news to the bad because it means that at some time in your future God will not say to you, as your loving father on earth did, "You idiot! How could you do such terrible things? I am very angry with you!", but instead will say something horribly, infinitely more terrifying: "I never knew you: depart from me" (Mt 7:23). Only a father who loves his son can be angry toward him. As long as God has wrath toward you, you have hope. When he ceases his wrath toward you, you are either in Heaven or Hell.

> He hath not dealt with us after our sins;
> nor rewarded us according to our iniquities.

The most foolish thing you could possibly ask for from God is justice.

But how can the God whose justice is part of His unchangeable essence relax and compromise His justice, pretend to ignore it, or tell Himself a little lie about who we are and what we deserve? He cannot. He is like the sun: He cannot become darkness. He cannot change Himself. But He can change us. He can give us something like sunblock (Christ is something like sunblock—the analogy is not perfect, but it is not wholly wrong, either), something that will change the relationship without changing Him. That something is Christ, who in His own person totally satisfies both justice and mercy. (Mercy is the form love takes when it meets sin.) For God cannot "turn off" His love any more than He can turn off His justice. His justice is like the intense heat of the sun, and His mercy is like the light of the sun, and the two are inseparable aspects of one and the same reality, even though one is threatening and the other consoling. They are separate in us but not in God.

If there is any priority in God's acts toward us, mercy must precede justice for the simple reason that His first act toward us is to create us; and we could not possibly deserve, by justice, to be created. Nothing can. What does not have existence cannot have anything else, including deservingness. It can only be sheer altruistic love, not justice, that motivates God to create us; and mercy is the form that that same love then later takes when it confronts our sin.

> For as the heaven is high above the earth,
> so great is his mercy toward them that fear him.
> As far as the east is from the west,
> so far hath he removed our transgressions from us.

I love how "primitive" David is. Instead of abstract principles, he gives concrete images. How great is God's mercy? Where are its limits? Look up, with your physical eyes, and you can see the answer written in the universe He created. How high is the sky? Where does it end? Where is the ceiling in the sky against which you will bump your head if you fly high enough? There is none. There is always more.

God created the sky to let us apprehend infinity with our eyes, since we could not comprehend it with our minds.

Our mercy is usually *less* than our justice, since our mercy is a partial relaxation of our justice. For instance, when a young boy breaks a window and cannot repair it or pay for it, his father fixes it but makes the boy clean it up and help with the repair. That is a partial relaxation of justice. Or when a judge tells the convicted felon that the law demands a fine of ten thousand dollars for his offense, but he will reduce the fine to five because that is all that the felon can pay, he is relaxing justice. But if he fined the felon the whole amount that the law demanded and then paid the fine out of his own pocket, that would be unrelaxed justice *and* unrelaxed mercy. (That actually happened once in court when the felon was the judge's son.)

God's mercy is infinite, like the heavens. No sin can exhaust the supply of God's mercy. The guilt of the greatest sin ever committed, the torture and murder of Almighty God, was swallowed up by the mercy of Christ, who prayed, "Father, forgive them; for they know not what they do" (Lk 23:34). No sin, but only the proud refusal to repent, can block God's forgiveness.

God's justice is definable, by law, but God's mercy is not definable by any law. When Peter asked Christ about the limits of mercy and forgiveness and said, "Lord, how oft shall my brother sin against me, and I forgive him? till seven times?" (Mt 18:21). Christ replied, "[No,] seventy times seven"—which meant, in an age of poor math skills, not "exactly 490 times", but, as a child would say, "zillions of times", an incalculably large number. Infinity. All the sins of the human race are like a grain of sand, and God's mercy is like the sea.

This mercy is offered to all sinners. All who "fear" God, i.e., who believe, trust, love, respect, worship, or say a fundamental Yes to God and His mercy receive it. Only those who refuse it do not get it. The light shines on all; some open their eyes to it, and some do not.

When do we get the light? As soon as we open our eyes. When do we receive God's grace? As soon as we believe it. ("Believe" and "receive" are identified in John 1:12.)

What is the essential work of God's mercy? The forgiveness of our sins, at the cost of His own life, on the Cross. And what does that forgiveness mean? It means more than merely a set of actions toward us—actions that help us rather than harm us—though it means that, too. It means more than merely a set of attitudes or intentions or feelings or desires or willings toward us—having benevolent rather than malevolent or wrathful attitudes—though it means that, too. It means something metaphysical, something ontological, not just something psychological or legal. It changes reality. It means really, truly, in objective fact, removing our sins from us. We pray, in the Mass, "Lamb of God, you [who] *take away* the sins of the world, have mercy on us." He actually, literally, takes our sins away from us. In technical, theological terms, he not only justifies us, He sanctifies us. He was called "Jesus", not merely because he would save us from the punishment due to our sins (what a selfish, mean, unholy idea that is!), but "thou shalt call his name JESUS: for he shall save his people from *their sins*" (Mt 1:21). His mercy is an objective reality, like fire, which makes cold things really hot, or like water, which makes dry things really wet, or like creation, which makes unreal things really real. God's merciful grace makes dirty souls clean.

His mercy is as high as the heaven above the earth. God removes our sins from us as far as the heaven is above the earth. Just how high is the heaven above the earth? Infinitely high, whether "the heaven" is taken to mean the physical firmament (which has no limit, as space has no wall around it) or the supernatural, spiritual dwelling of God. God's mercy is as limitlessly far above the earth vertically as the east is limitlessly far from the west horizontally; that is how far He removes our sins from us.

How far is the east from the west? Is there any limit, any line, any wall between east and west? None. No matter how far you travel east, you do not travel west. No matter how far you travel west, you do not travel east. East and west are as opposite as being and nonbeing, light and darkness, good and evil, holiness and sin. It is exactly as far (infinitely) from the east to the west as it is from the heaven to the earth. No matter how far you travel up, you do not travel down. And because His mercy is as high as the heaven over the earth, therefore it removes our sins as far from us as the east is from the west. The two images are identical: they both mean infinity.

Where does God send our sins when He removes them from us? Into forgetfulness? That is not absolute; remembrance may overcome it. Into the past? That still lives in the present, in remembering. He sends our sins to Hell, to eternal and absolute exile from all that is alive and present and good. And if we identify with our sins, we must accompany them; and if we disavow our sins, by repentance, He sends us to Heaven and our sins to Hell, and between the two "there is a great gulf fixed" (Lk 16:26), so that there is no common world containing both; there is nothing in common between Heaven and Hell, no bridge between either one and the other, no chance for anyone in Heaven to slip into Hell or anyone in Hell to slip into Heaven.

> Like as a father pitieth his children,
> so the LORD pitieth them that fear him.

How does a father pity his children? Ask any good father.

In Elizabethan English, "pity" means "active compassion". It does not have the connotation that "pity" has in modern English, in which "pity" is a mere feeling, something passive, not an action. "Pity" in our culture also has negative connotations of sadness, helplessness, and weakness or else supercilious condescension. Here, "pity", like "compassion", is an essential aspect of *agape*, *caritas*, or "active love".

In this verse, the poet turns from two cosmological images (vertical and horizontal) of the distance God sets between us and our sins to a human image of the relation between the forgiver (the father) and the forgiven (his children). The point of the cosmological image is the infinite distance, the infinite difference. Here the point of the human image is a proportional similarity. Insofar as a human father is a remote image of the Heavenly Father, his pity to his children is a remote image of the Heavenly Father's pity to us.

The similarity works "upside down", so to speak, that is, in the opposite way than the way we think. God is not literally like a human father, but there is a real analogy between the two because human fathers are a little like God. "Call no man your father upon the earth" (Mt 23:9) does not mean that human fathers are not really fathers, but that they are pale copies, shadows, or symbols of the Fatherhood of God.

That verse illustrates what Saint Thomas says about our language about God: that we have to choose between literally true negatives and only analogically or metaphorically or symbolically true positives. We know that God is not anything limited. For instance, He is not temporal but e-ternal, i.e., not temporal. And of course God is not mortal. And this is literal knowledge because we know literally what is limited and what is mortal. But we do not know literally those positive divine attributes of eternity and infinite life that exclude time and death. Our literal knowledge of God is only negative. And our positive knowledge of God is only analogical, not literal. For instance, we know that God is more like a saint than a sinner, more like a shepherd than a sheep, and more like a living thing than a dead thing; but this is a "like" rather than an "is"; that is, it is not literal. For saints, shepherds, and other living things are temporal and mortal, while God is eternal.

God's knowledge does not conform to or copy things, like a scientist or a photographer, but designs and constitutes things, like an artist or a novelist. As he knew us into existence, he knows us into "pitiability", into compassionability, into lovability. His love creates and recreates its objects (us). The point is so central that it is worth pursuing, for it is at the heart of the thing that is at the heart of all of religion, namely, divine *agape* love. It is God's love for us, as well as his knowledge of us (those two things are one thing in Him), that make us lovable, that cause our worth and value and lovability, rather than our lovability causing his love for us. And the practical point of this difficult theological truth is that we are called on to do the same thing he does: to love the unlovable and thereby make them lovable rather than to love only the lovable or to love them only because they are lovable. That is the difference between all the natural loves and supernatural love. That is the essence of *agape*, which is the essence of God.

Even if we do not (or even cannot) understand how this can be so, we can know, from His own revelation, that it is so. And we can live it even if we do not understand it.

We are "flesh", i.e., weak, both morally and metaphysically. We are fickle, and we are finite. We are tempted

to sin (soul-death) and subjected to its necessary consequence (body-death), since soul and body always share
the same fate, the fate of the single person who is both
soul and body, as a single symphony is both beauty and
sound or as a single book is both words and meaning. To
change either one of those two dimensions is to change
the other. You cannot change the words without changing the meaning, and you cannot change the meaning
without changing the words. Our bodies are our words,
and our souls are our meanings.

> As for man, his days are as grass:
> as a flower of the field, so he flourisheth.
> For the wind passeth over it, and it is gone;
> and the place thereof shall know it no more.

We are blades of grass, we are flowers—blades of grass that
think, flowers that think. It takes only a chill wind or an
invisibly tiny virus to kill us. The universe that does not
think always kills its flowers (us) that do think. And there is
no return, no reincarnation: "the place thereof shall know
it no more."

Notice how concrete the poet is. He does not talk
about an abstraction like "mortality" or even "death". He
talks about grass and flowers and wind and empty places.
Poetry is much more concrete than philosophy, theology,
science, or ideology.

"Dust thou art, and unto dust shalt thou return." Once
a year a priest reminds us of this fundamental truth when
he puts ashes on our foreheads on Ash Wednesday. The
medieval Christians reminded themselves much more
often than that. *Memento mori*, "remember death", was
a popular slogan—popular, not because it brought happiness, but because it brought wisdom. They lived in a

wisdom culture; we live in a happiness culture. Our fundamental popular liturgy, our "hello", is "How are you?"
and the required answer is "Fine!"—even if your dog just
died, your mother-in-law is coming to live with you, and
the IRS is going to audit your tax return. Our popular
liturgy is a lie. No one is really, truly, deeply happy and
"fine". Just as a culture that lives in the denial of death is
not a culture of life, a culture that denies unhappiness
is not a culture of happiness.

What is the alternative to the popular modern liturgical greeting "How are you? / Fine"? It is the liturgical
greeting in the Mass: *Dominus vobiscum / Et cum spiritu tuo*.
"The Lord be with you / And with your spirit." Notice
how abstract the modern liturgy is and how concrete the
ancient one is. Notice how subjective the modern liturgy
is and how objective the ancient one is. Notice how concrete and objective the Psalmist's talk about death is: grass,
flowers, wind, and an empty place. Death is very concrete,
and that is why God's solution to it is very concrete. It is
Resurrection, and in the Nicene Creed the Greek words
that we translate "the resurrection of the dead" (*anastasis
nekron*) mean literally "the standing up of the corpse". You
cannot get more concrete than that. Ask Lazarus.

A Judaeo-Christian culture is a culture of true happiness
because it prays, "Teach us to number our days, that we
may apply our hearts unto wisdom" (Ps 90:12). Without
memento mori, there is no wisdom, and without wisdom,
there is no true happiness.

Our secular culture lies about death. No one dies any
more, they just "pass away". Ironically, such a culture of
the denial of death is what Pope Saint John Paul II called
a "culture of death". A Christian culture like the Middle
Ages, which remembered death, was a culture of life, a
culture that sang (in the words of the old oratorio "Open

Our Eyes"): "Thou hast made death glorious and triumphant, for through its portals we enter into the presence
of the Living God." Our modern secular culture will not
confess that premise, and therefore it cannot experience
that "glorious and triumphant" conclusion.

> But the mercy of the LORD is from everlasting to
>   everlasting upon them that fear him,
> and his righteousness unto children's children;
> To such as keep his covenant,
> and to those that remember his commandments to
>   do them.

The powerful word here is "but". Man's mortality is certain, *but* God's mercy is even more certain. Man is not
everlasting, *but* God and His mercy are. Man is fickle and
untrustable, *but* God is faithful (*emeth*) and trustable. Pity
those who have faith in faith rather than in God. Faith in
faith in what? Without God, faith is a hall of mirrors that
endlessly reflect other mirrors.

Truth, fidelity (*emeth*), or trustability is, with us, usually
contrasted with mercy as bone and flesh, as the hard vs.
the soft. We contrast head and heart, truth and love, the
eternal and the temporal, the objective and the subjective,
the tough and the tender. God alone unites them. Truth
and justice and trustability and everlastingness are like a
rock: they will not soften. Without the rock to lean on, we
lean on wind. But we also need the soft, the merciful, the
compassionate. God perfectly unites these two most fundamental values. "Mercy and truth are met together; righteousness and peace have kissed each other" (Ps 85:10).

How? By Christ, who alone perfectly and completely
and finally reveals the nature of God; by the Incarnation;
by the fact that truth and righteousness (justice, the "hard"

aspect of God) have sprung "out of the earth" (of Mary's womb) as well as "down from heaven" (by the Incarnation) (Ps 85:11). And, correlatively, by the fact that love and compassion (the "soft" aspect of God) have looked "down from heaven", i.e., revealed themselves as the eternal nature of the God of Heaven (by the Incarnation) as well as having sprung "out of the earth" of our human need. You could diagram this joining of right (truth) and left (love) and of up (Heaven) and down (earth) by a Cross.

And that mercy, when it reaches down to redeem us, does not merely reveal an attitude or an act of God, so that God just writes off our sins rather than changing us, so that the *relationship* is changed from condemnation to justification, but *we* are still, in Luther's words, "a sack of shit covered with white snow". Instead, God's mercy reaches down and touches us, and it changes everything in us and in our lives. Everything! "Behold, I make all things new" (Rev 21:5).

And since faith, in Scripture, is always faith-in-action, or fidelity (*emeth*), and not just intellectual belief, the Psalmist describes the faith-full as those who actively "keep" His covenant, which is God's spiritual marriage to man. That covenant is the meaning of the Law, the Commandments. The Law is not a set of abstract rules, like Platonic Ideas; they are a concrete *covenant*, a spiritual marriage, between the two most concrete entities in our experience: our God and ourselves, the "great I AM" and the human "I", His image.

That concreteness is the reason why the Psalmist does not speak of those who "obey" His Commandments but of those who "keep" them, who live them, as one lives a marriage rather than "obeys" it. A marriage is not merely a set of rules. It is a concrete, committed relationship between two persons. It is even more than that: it is not just something two people invent or do; it is, first of all, a real thing in itself, like an elephant. You do not have to climb onto it, but if you do, you are no longer in yourself, you are on the elephant. Thus Scripture says that husband and wife become "one flesh", one body, one real human entity, without ceasing to be two persons. A family is not just relationship; a family is a body; a family is a citizen; a family is a *thing*, like an elephant. It is one thing, yet its oneness does not abolish its members' individuality any more than God's oneness abolishes the individuality of the three Persons of the Trinity. Like the Trinity, the family is both "I" and "We".

> The LORD hath prepared his throne in the heavens;
> and his kingdom ruleth over all.

This verse sounds different. There is now a change from mercy to glory, from prayer to praise. It is not a second psalm tacked onto the first, but the natural response to the insight into the glory of that mercy. The "throne" and "rule" and "kingdom" spoken of here are not mere power but love, not mere justice but mercy. Mercy has power. Right has might. Love is not weak. Love conquers. Love "shall cover the multitude of sins" (1 Pet 4:8). Love *whups* sin. Love also whups death.

> Bless the LORD, ye his angels, that excel in strength,
> that do his commandments, hearkening unto the
>   voice of his word.
> Bless ye the LORD, all ye his hosts;
> ye ministers of his, that do his pleasure.

That news about God's mercy is so good that the Psalmist next calls on all creation to join the praise, especially those with the highest nature and mind and will and voice, the angels. Since they are far above us, they praise God far more powerfully than we. Since we are far below them, we praise Him far more feebly than they. But we praise Him together with them. We invoke them to give God the praise He deserves, since we cannot do it as well as they can. They cannot give God *all* the praise He deserves—no one can do that but God Himself—but they can come much closer to it than we can, and they are happy to "stand in for" us, to do for us their praise in our name. And they are more than willing to answer that prayer.

> Bless the LORD, all his works
> in all places of his dominion:
> Bless the LORD, O my soul.

The last verse of this psalm is like the last psalm in the Psalter, Psalm 150, which concludes, "Let every thing that hath breath praise the LORD." (And everything does have breath, life, or being. Everything acts. Everything does praise God, even the dust.) All of creation is called on to praise God, for nothing less will do. The Psalmist is merely asking all of creation to do now what it in fact does at every moment.

For us to join this great chorus is a foretaste of Heaven. While on earth, we can know, by faith (faith is a knowing) that everything else is singing this song of praise to its Creator; but when we actually join the song, that is like being *in* a great choir, inside the music, rather than outside it in the audience.

The only things in the universe that have a choice to join or not to join in this song are human souls. Therefore David, with all his soul, commands his soul to join the song of the universe. (The soul commands itself: that is a good definition of free will or free choice.) We need to do the same, and we need to remember to do it many times a day. That is why we have to keep coming back to psalms like this one many times. We have spiritual Attention Deficit Disorder.

Psalm 19

"The heavens declare the glory of God"

This was one of C. S. Lewis' favorite psalms. I was struck by that fact when I saw how much it was marked up in his prayer book (in the Wade Collection at Wheaton College).

It is about the two ways God reveals Himself: naturally and supernaturally, in the Book of Nature and the Book of Scripture (He wrote both books!), especially in the sun and in the Law. The sun is for us at the center of His natural revelation, while the Law is at the center of His supernatural revelation to His chosen people, the Jews, His collective prophet to the world.

Jews in modern times are not known for their love of nature or for Romantic poetry about the land, largely because between A.D. 70 and 1948 they *had* no land. During the Diaspora, or dispersion, they were driven to jobs remote from the soil (jewelry, finance, science, literature, psychiatry, law).

Because the Jews knew the transcendent Creator more clearly than any pagans did, they emptied nature of the pagan gods who inhabited it. This demythologization of nature allowed nature to cease being God's home and become God's art, God's second book of revelation, together with Scripture. Thus in Psalm 19, the sun (in God's "second book") becomes the natural symbol of the light of the Law (in God's "first book"), which both declares the glory of God and searches and cleanses the heart.

Those pagans who came the closest to monotheism naturally focused on the sun: mainly Akhenaton in Egypt and Socrates in Greece. The latter believed he had been inspired by Apollo, the god of the sun, and he spent the last night of his life composing a hymn to Apollo. (Yet Socrates could not honestly confess, during his trial, that he believed in any of "the gods of the state", including Apollo, i.e., believed what the state believed about them. Because of this, he was executed for "atheism".) The sun was and is the source of all natural physical light and heat. If you are never even *tempted* to worship the sun, there is something missing in you: you have lost your natural instincts (as most technologized cultures have).

There are two parts to this psalm because God has revealed Himself in two ways (natural and supernatural). The first, God's revelation in nature, is insufficient because it does not include morality. Nature has no morality. It manifests great beauty and intelligence but not moral goodness. It cares not whether you are holy or unholy; it gives birth and life to you even if you are unholy, and it gives pain and death to you even if you are holy. Thus the Law is a more complete revelation of God, not just of His mind, but also of His will. This Law is known to all by conscience (which is also part of natural revelation), but it is known in a clearer and more definitive way to the Jews (and to the world through them) by the Ten Commandments.

Yet even this most complete revelation of God's will in the Law is insufficient to heal us and save us and bless us with deep joy because we do not keep it. God's Law is our X ray, not our surgery. It shows up our sin. In a sense it is the bad news, not the good news. When Saint Paul speaks of these two universal natural revelations of God, in nature and in conscience, in Romans, his point is not optimistic (that we have this great light about God) but pessimistic (that we have sinned against the light). That very light is what makes us responsible.

> For the wrath [justice] of God is revealed from heaven against all ungodliness [irreligion] and unrighteousness [immorality] of men, who hold the truth ["hold" it in the sense both of knowing it and of suppressing it, or holding it down] in unrighteousness. Because that which may be known of God is manifest in them; for God hath shewed it unto them. For the invisible things of him from the creation of the world are clearly seen, being understood by the things that are made [nature], even his eternal power and Godhead; so that they are without excuse: Because that, when they knew God, they glorified him not as God, neither were thankful; but became vain in their imaginations, and their foolish heart was darkened. Professing themselves to be wise, they became fools. (Rom 1:18–22)

So even the three revelations implied in this psalm, viz., nature, conscience, and the Law that God revealed to the Jews, are insufficient. They do not give us hope. In fact, they do the opposite: they give us despair because we have sinned against the knowledge we have. Only Christ gives us hope, for as sinners our only hope is in God's mercy. Fortunately, even many who do not know Christ as Savior—Jews and Muslims—know they are sinners and know their hope is in God's mercy.

This psalm is not about Christ explicitly; yet it is the necessary foundation for faith in Christ. Without the natural revelations of God in nature and conscience, and without the supernatural Jewish revelation of the Law, we would not clearly know either God's perfection or our sinfulness. And without that knowledge, Christ would be meaningless; He would be an answer to a question we had never asked: "What must I do to be saved?" Thus

this psalm is Christian in a fundamental and necessary way,
even though not directly and explicitly. It is about the
underground foundation of the Christian cathedral.

> The heavens declare the glory of God;
> and the firmament sheweth his handywork.

Wonder and gratitude are the first and necessary seedbed
of all religion. These two spiritual instincts are our natural
response to the script God wrote in the stars. Think of
Emerson's great thought-experiment: "If the stars should
appear but once in a thousand years...." Many an atheist had his first religious experience when contemplating
the stars. Science supplies more and more reasons for that
instinctive wonder and gratitude. For the more we know
about the universe through our science, the more intri-
cately and delicately designed for human life it shows itself
to be. The windows of opportunity for human life evolv-
ing were arranged with nearly impossible accuracy and
perfection. For instance, if the temperature of the prime-
val fireball a millionth of a second after the Big Bang had
been a millionth of a degree hotter or colder, the carbon
molecule, which is the basis for all life, could never have
come to be. There are hundreds of such tiny windows of
opportunity for life, that is, for us. What is most incredible
of all is our blasé indifference to this heavenly script that
nearly screams to us that there is a supernatural Voice singing the stars into being as notes in a perfect song.

> Day unto day uttereth speech,
> and night unto night sheweth knowledge.

The day utters this poem, not to the next day (for the next
day cannot read it), but to us. The night does not show this
knowledge to the next night (nights have no reason), but

to us. Each day and each night the song is sung again. It is continuous; it never stops. The book is always there for us to read. Unless we act like dumb animals who chew a book instead of reading it, what we read there is *logos*, that is, "speech" and "knowledge".

> There is no speech nor language where their voice is
>   not heard.
> Their line is gone out through all the earth, and their
>   words to the end of the world.

Not only through all time but also through all space, in all places, this song is sung. The universal language of nature overarches all particular languages and cultures on earth, as the sky overarches all nations and tribes. "For the invisible things of him from the creation of the world are clearly seen, being understood by the things that are made, even his eternal power and Godhead; so that they are without excuse" (Rom 1:20).

This universal song has a "line", or script, that is, "lyrics", as well as melody. It appeals to our head as well as to our heart. The script is as intelligent as the melody is beautiful. God manifests both His mind and His heart, both His science and His art, both His truth and His beauty, in nature. The only person who could be ignorant of this universal revelation would be either a brute with no head or a viper with no heart. Or (worse) a fool who suppressed both his head and his heart.

Next comes one of the most memorable natural images in Scripture:

> In them hath he set a tabernacle for the sun,
> Which is as a bridegroom coming out of his chamber,
>   and rejoiceth as a strong man to run a race.

The sun, like a god, has a tabernacle, a holy place. It is not Heaven, but it is "the heavens". Today we call that holy place simply "outer space". We see it as empty. Our ancestors saw it as full—not of molecules, but of the glory of God. We see "space" as a thing—an empty thing. Our ancestors used the word "space" simply as a three-dimensional aspect of material things. Things contained their "space". For us, "space" contains all things.

Of course the sun is not a god. But it *is* an icon of God. It is a very natural mistake to worship the sun, like the great Egyptian monotheist Akhenaton. We moderns make a much worse mistake than that. If you see the sun as nothing but a large ball of hydrogen and helium, you have sunk below even idolatry. Only if you see the sun as something more, something that is only *made of* hydrogen and helium, can you rise to the heresy of idolatry. If you sink below it, you are not even a good pagan.

Or else—far worse—perhaps you do not love the sunlight, because it exposes you. Even though no one prefers physical darkness to light (except when they want to hide their crimes), we all at some times prefer comfortable spiritual darkness to uncomfortable spiritual light, and some prefer it habitually. Welcome to the universe's planet-wide insane asylum, which you entered on the day you were conceived, son of Adam or daughter of Eve.

The poet proceeds to two human images for the sun, which is itself a subhuman image for the superhuman God. The sun, he says, is like a bridegroom and like a racer. These are personifications, i.e., treating as a person that which is less than a person. Personification in the opposite direction is impossible because there is nothing that is greater than a person. Theists do not personify God; pantheists de-personify Him. Sometimes images can work upside down, so to speak, as de-personifications, treating a person as a thing or an animal ("he is a fox", "she is a snake", "he is a clod", "she is a star").

All this works only because all things are full of analogies between higher and lower links on "the great chain of being", rungs on Jacob's ladder. Christ is, of course, the ultimate Jacob's ladder (compare Jn 1:51 with Gen 28:12); but nature is one, too. Our minds can climb up the ladder God put into nature (Rom 1:20), but our whole souls can climb up the ladder God sent down in Christ. In our fallen state, that first ladder, the ladder of natural knowledge, condemns us ("so that they are without excuse"—Rom 1:20). Only the second ladder saves us, because it is bigger than nature, or super-natural. The little ladder leads to the larger, latter ladder.

The sun is like a bridegroom. The bridegroom emerges from his chamber (bedroom) victorious, young, healthy, robust, virile, and fertile. The sun, like God, is not our wife but our husband. We are his bride, not he ours. He impregnates us—he gives us new life—we do not impregnate him. He enlightens us, we do not enlighten him. This is not male chauvinism; it is almost female chauvinism: spiritually, we are the bride, we are all women to God.

Thus the pronoun for the true God must be a "he", not a "she", (or, even worse, an "it") *if* it is the true God who is revealing Himself to us rather than we who are revealing ourselves to Him. The God of the Bible knows better than we do how to speak about Himself! That is, *if* this is the God who comes to us from objective reality rather than from our own ideology or imagination or preferences. The latter is a god we can imagine and, therefore, a god we "can feel comfortable with". Divine revelation's aim is truth, not comfort or political correctness. That is why the true God is always spoken of as "he", never "she", throughout the whole of original, orthodox, faithful Jewish, Christian, and Islamic tradition. The pronoun is

neither a projection of our traditional cultural male chauvinism (which is real, and deplorable) nor an accidental
and dispensable human invention. It is a divine revelation.

The sun is like a racer as well as a bridegroom. The
racer is also young, strong, healthy, robust, active, virile,
athletic, a competitor, a fighter, and a conqueror. No one
can catch him, even in thought. God is so fast that He is
omnipresent, in all places at once. "Run, run, as fast as you
can; you can't catch him, he's the gingerbread man."

> His going forth is from the end of the heaven,
> and his circuit unto the ends of it:
> and there is nothing hid from the heat thereof.

Light is ubiquitous. Even if it begins in one place, it
expands into all places. A telescope sensitive and powerful
enough, placed on a planet two thousand light years away,
would register the light waves that bounced off Jesus' face.
Seeing outward into space is also seeing backward into
past time. If the sun exploded now, we would not see it or
feel it for about eight minutes. The Psalmist did not know
modern astronomy and physics, of course, but his clear
point is that there is no place that is not subject to the sun,
i.e., to light, i.e., to truth, i.e., to God.

Yet a beam of this light moves in time from one place to
another and visits one place at one time and another place
at another time. However, the different places it visits do
not change the light; rather, the light changes the different
places it visits. Although it moves, our places and times
do not determine and define its movement; its movement
determines and defines our places and times. (This is even
true scientifically in a way, for the speed of light is the
universal constant.) God is not subject to time; He subjects
time to Himself. He is active and dynamic, but not changing. Unchanged Himself, He changes all things.

The sun's circuit is "from the end of the heaven" and "unto the ends of it". But there is no end to what the Psalmist calls "the heavens", which is what we call "space". As with numbers, you can always add to upness or downness, eastness or westness. The world, like the universe, is round. There is no edge to space, no wall at the end of the world.

However, there is an edge to time. It is called death. There is also an opposite edge to time. It is called creation, or "the Big Bang". For each of us, it is the moment of conception. Souls are created, not evolved.

He (the sun) moves from end to end, east to west, excluding nothing and no one. He is universal, or "catholic" or "inclusive".

He gives two things: light and heat. Nothing can hide from either God's light (mind, truth, knowledge) or heat (will, desire, love). These two things that distinguish us from the beasts, knowledge of truth and love of goodness, are finite images of infinite divine attributes. Physical light gives us knowledge of physical things, and spiritual light gives us knowledge of spiritual things, ultimately of God. Heat gives us physical life and is an image for spiritual love, which compared with physical love is a passion that burns more, not less. Every physical passion, like the sun, has a highest temperature, a measurable limit to its heat; the fire of divine love (*agape*) does not.

The last line of this verse is the connection between the sun and the Law and, thus, the two parts of this psalm: nothing is "hid" from either. Think of the burning sun in a desert climate. Everything is exposed and defenseless before it.

> The law of the LORD is perfect, converting the soul:
> the testimony of the LORD is sure, making wise the
>   simple.

And now, suddenly, without warning or transitional words, the poet moves from the sun to the Law. For he is writing this psalm to tell us something about the Law, not about the sun. His point is not primarily to expand our understanding and appreciation of the sun by showing us that it is like the Law (though that might be a by-product), but to expand our understanding and appreciation of the Law by showing us that it is like the sun. In fact, the implication is that God invented the sun precisely to show us what the Law is like.

The first two properties of this Law, analogous to those of the sun, are "perfect" and "pure". They are almost the same thing. The sun is simply *sun* all the way through. It is perfectly sunny, purely sunny. It is not like a compound but like an element. It has no parts, no cracks, no conflicts. The Law is like this. Even though it has ten "commandments", it is one Law. To break any Commandment is to break the single relationship with the single Commander. As God is wholly one, our relationship with Him must be wholly one: life or death, good or evil, light or darkness, the blessing or the curse, yes or no. There is no room for compromise. A divided mind and heart is unwisdom and unholiness. An undivided heart and mind is wisdom and holiness. One of the properties of holiness is wholeness, or oneness, because to be holy is to be like God (Lev 20:26), and God is One.

This Law converts those who are "simple" in the wrong way (simpleminded, stupid, unwise) into people who are "simple" in the right way (simple in will, loving God with their whole heart, wise). Kierkegaard wrote a book with the profound and beautiful title *Purity of Heart Is to Will One Thing*.

> The statutes of the LORD are right, rejoicing the heart:
> the commandment of the LORD is pure, enlightening
> the eyes.

The next two properties of the Law are that it is "right" and that it is "pure". "Right" is a moral word. It means "righteous". "Pure" here is a metaphysical word. It means "one, perfect, unmixed, and undivided".

The "rightness" of the Law gives the "heart" (will and desire and love) what it both wants and needs, namely, joy, or "rejoicing". Only an evil heart would rejoice at an evil law, a wrong law; a good heart would rejoice at a good law, a right law. Thus those who impugn God's Law as "repressive" or "dehumanizing" reveal nothing about the Law but much about themselves. The Law of God is thus a test of our heart.

The "purity" (or perfection) of the Law mentioned in the second line also gives to the mind (here symbolized by "the eyes") what it wants and needs, namely, "enlightenment", or truth. The same two qualities—goodness and truth, love and wisdom—are manifested again and again by God's works, because they manifest qualities in God. That is why they perfect and satisfy the two main powers in the human soul that constitute "the image of God", the two powers that no mere animal has, namely, the mind or intellect and the moral heart and will.

These two perfections are the two things that nearly everyone who has had a near-death experience or an out-of-body experience and has caught a glimpse of the next life says he learned are the only two things that you can take with you after death, the only two things you really need, and the two things the "Being of Light" whom they meet gives you: love and wisdom, goodness and truth, the good of the heart and the good of the mind.

> The fear of the LORD is clean, enduring for ever:
> the judgments of the LORD are true and righteous
>   altogether.

The "fear of the Lord", i.e., respectful love and loving respect, is almost identical with the "fear" of the Law, since the Law, for the Jew, was the most important and direct connection with the Lord, the soul's umbilical cord to Him. That is why the Psalmist loves the Law, even though its perfection shows him up as a sinner: the love of the Law is the love of the Lord because the Law is the face of the Lord, the heart of the Lord, the will of the Lord.

This "fear" is said to be "clean", that is, unmixed, pure, absolutely right. That is why it is "enduring for ever": because what is not perfectly "clean" but mixed can be unmixed, but what is clean and pure and one cannot. Compounds can be dissolved; elements cannot.

In the next line, the Law is called the "judgments" of the Lord. These are not God's judgments of human beings after they have obeyed or disobeyed the Law, but these "judgments" are the laws themselves, the Ten Commandments. God's "judging" here is not His response to our actions but His willing the Law. In legislating the laws, He is acting like Congress, not like the Court.

God's Law is perfect ("true and righteous altogether") because its Author is perfect. The Law reveals the face, the character, the personality, the heart and will of the Lawgiver. It is not just abstract concepts or truths or ideas; it is the personality of the concrete Divine Person. The biblical book of Leviticus makes that very clear: the reason for obeying the Law is given by God repeatedly in Leviticus, along with the Law itself: "Ye shall be holy: for I the LORD your God am holy." To be good is to be real; to be holy is to be like the paradigm and standard for realness, viz., God. Sanctity is the perfect sanity. Ethics is the ultimate metaphysics.

And, therefore, to be evil is to be unreal, to lose your being, your identity, your self, your "I", your image of

God, your personhood, your life, your soul. "For what shall it profit a man, if he shall gain the whole world, and lose his own soul?" (Mk 8:36).

> More to be desired are they than gold, yea, than
>   much fine gold:
> sweeter also than honey and the honeycomb.

Here is the ultimate reason for loving the Law, why contemplating it is the Psalmist's "delight" and "sweeter than honey". The reason is its beauty. The Law is *beautiful*. The Law describes the most beautiful thing in the world, a saint.

Spiritual beauty is more beautiful than physical beauty because physical beauty reveals, expresses, and symbolizes spiritual beauty, not vice versa. There is much more in the spirit than the body can reveal. A human being is like that stable in Bethlehem: there is in that stable something bigger than the whole world. It is bigger on the inside than on the outside. So are we.

To reverse the image, the body is really in the soul rather than the soul in the body, as the material setting of a play is in the play. It is the bodily, material aspect or part of the play, of the play's identity and meaning, of the play's "soul". It is not the other way round: the play's identity, meaning, or soul is not a part of its material setting.

The psalm sees the Law as beautiful. Beauty is the child of truth and goodness. It is both a cause and an effect of their unity. It connects truth and goodness, understanding and love, for it is the beauty of what is understood and contemplated that generates the love of it. That is why there is no sin in Heaven, even though our free will is not taken away: because the Vision is "beatific", because seeing the Face of God removes the ignorance that is a part of (though not an excuse for) all temptation. In Heaven,

everything will appear as it really is: what is truly beautiful
will appear as beautiful, not ugly or onerous; and what is
truly ugly will appear as ugly, not as beautiful and tempting. Thus in Heaven the Law will look like gold and taste
like honey. The psalm is a tiny fortaste of Heaven.

By the way, gold, honey, and the sun—three of the
most prominent images the Psalmist uses for God's Law—
are all yellow. Among the colors, it seems to be a natural
icon. I suspect that people whose favorite color is yellow
(they are few) are very often innocent, happy, and holy
people. (That does not mean that there is not also effective iconography in other colors: white for purity, green
for life, red for passion, blue for truth, purple for wonder, black for mystery. I do not see any holy symbolism
in pink.)

> Moreover by them is thy servant warned:
> and in keeping of them there is great reward.

The Psalmist now adds two more reasons for loving the
Law as something beautiful and sweet. The first is that
it warns us of evil, ugliness, misery, and folly. Warning
signs are usually ugly because they are pictures of the
ugly thing that we are being warned against. Yet they
are beautiful, or at least desirable, because being freed
from pain and ugliness is almost as joyful as being given
pleasure and beauty.

The second reason is that just as the Law warns us
against punishments, it promises us rewards. Even if it
did not, it would be beautiful, even if "virtue is its own
reward" were the whole story. It is not only the rewards,
or even primarily the rewards, that ought to motivate us.
We should do the right thing, first of all, simply because
it is the right thing. But there are also not only rewards

but "great" rewards: Heaven, mystical experience, ecstasy, beholding the Face of God—the word "great" is not nearly great enough for that.

> Who can understand his errors?
> cleanse thou me from secret faults.

So far, the only negative note in the psalm is the word "warned", where the negative is not described but implied. Everything has been "good news". Now comes the "bad news". We are prone to sin against the Law. The Law is there because of that. There will be no need for the Law in Heaven. We need the sun's light because we have darkness, and we need the Law of Goodness because we have evil: in fact, not only sins but also "presumptuous" sins (mentioned in the next verse).

In this verse, the sins are not "presumptuous" but only "errors" and "secret faults". This probably means, not sins that we keep secret from others by lying, but sins that we are in ignorance of in ourselves. These are not only not "presumptuous", but they are "secret" rather than known, so that they are not clearly conscious or deliberate; so although they are sins, they are only venial sins, things like our purely spontaneous rather than deliberate lust, laziness, selfishness, insensitivity, impatience, anger, envy, or resentment, which arise before we can censor them. But they are habitual and harmful, like all sins.

In the next verse, by contrast, the sins are mortal. Presumption and despair are the two sins that are worse than any other because they imply "no repentance", and no other sin implies that. Presumption is almost another word for pride, and that is the greatest sin, the devil's sin.

The very fact that the Psalmist is worried about his "secret sins" means that sin does not have dominion over him. This negative note is really positive. It is humility, which is the first and most necessary virtue: to admit that we lack virtue. (Similarly, the first wisdom is to admit that we lack wisdom. Only fools think they are wise; the wise know they are fools. Only great sinners think they are saints; all the saints know they are sinners.)

And so the Psalmist prays to God for the grace that can come only from Him, not us. We cannot keep ourselves from either "secret sins" or "presumptuous sins" without God's supernatural grace. Brother Lawrence, in *The Practice of the Presence of God*, says that after he sins he says to God, "See? That's what I shall always do when You do not give me the grace", and then gets up from his fall and begins again.

> Keep back thy servant also from presumptuous sins;
> let them not have dominion over me:
> then shall I be upright,
> and I shall be innocent from the great transgression.

The Psalmist is not so proud and foolish as to think that he will become perfectly innocent in this life, but he hopes to be at least innocent of "the great transgression". He knows God will not keep him from all sins (that would be supremely dangerous because that would tempt him to the worst sin of all, pride!), so he prays only for being kept from "presumptuous sins" and from "the great transgression" (which are probably the same thing: unrepentant pride). He knows that sins will continue to oppress him, but he hopes, and prays, that they will not have "dominion" over him.

That is the difference between venial and mortal sin (the terminology is specifically Catholic, but the point is scriptural: see 1 Jn 5:16–17), between (1) keeping our freedom of choice even though we have lost our freedom from sin, our innocence, like Adam and Eve, and (2) losing not only our innocence but also our very freedom of choice, like Judas. It is the difference between (1) being guilty of evil and (2) addictive enslavement to evil. They are more similar than different, in at least three ways: all sin separates us from God, whether temporarily or eternally; we cannot free ourselves by ourselves from either, so that God's grace alone can free us from both; and all sin is addictive and is like a disease to our freedom, but mortal sin is death to our freedom.

Yet, paradoxically, only a *free* and knowing choice to commit a deed that is a "grave evil" qualifies as a sin that is "mortal", that *destroys* our freedom. The only thing that can take away our freedom is not any other enemy, not anything external to our own will, not suffering or death or even Satan or Hell itself, but only our own free choice to sell ourselves into slavery.

There are three conditions for a mortal sin: serious matter, full knowledge, and free consent. Without full knowledge of the fact that the choice is both sinful and mortal and without full free consent in the will, even "serious matter" does not alone make an act a mortal sin that kills the supernatural life in the soul. If we are ignorant of the fact, or if we most deeply will not to do it rather than to do it when we struggle with it (which is something God alone can know with certainty), it is not mortal to us, even though it is seriously harmful and dangerous. It is dangerous especially because it naturally leads to more, deeper, and more enslaving repetitions. Thus the worst thing about venial sins is that they are "gateway drugs" to mortal sins. But to be in mortal sin, to be on our way to Hell, we must freely and knowingly sell ourselves into slavery. Neither God nor Satan damn

a soul; only the soul itself can do it. But when done, it
is done, and freedom is gone. A slave cannot escape any
more. He is chained.

If you sincerely struggle and honestly worry about mortal sin, you are not in the state of mortal sin—yet. Go (if
you are a Catholic) to confession quickly. God does not
tell you with certainty when you are in mortal sin, but
He does tell you with certainty when you are forgiven. It
is in a certain little box, apparently confining, but really
releasing us from our confinement (for sin is like a prison).
In that little box a miracle happens: Adam goes in, and
Jesus comes out. It is one of the two places Satan hates
and fears more than any other in the world. The other is
also a box-like thing, an altar, where bread goes in and
Jesus comes out.

> Let the words of my mouth, and the meditation of
>   my heart,
>   be acceptable in thy sight, O LORD, my strength,
>   and my redeemer.

This is not a mere afterthought, a postscript. It is in a
sense the most important verse of all because it takes all
the previous verses and subjects them to God's scrutiny
and judgment. The Psalmist is saying, in effect, "I don't
know what nonsense and folly I have spoken; only You
do. I let You decide that, and I want Your judgment and
Your will to be done, not mine, on everything, including
these very words."

The distinction between "the words of my mouth" and
"the meditation of my heart" is important. The Psalmist
does not excuse himself in the foolish way we so often do
by saying something like "My mouth may have spoken
the wrong words, but please take the deeper thoughts and

desires of my heart as what I really mean and judge me by that." It is almost the opposite for him, for he is more deeply suspicious of his heart than of his words. As he should be if he has the wisdom and humility to know himself as he is. Hard as it is to control our tongue (Jas 3:3–8), it is even harder to control our heart (Jer 17:9).

We have a great advantage over the Psalmist here. We know that the Psalmist's words are divinely inspired; he probably did not know that when he wrote them. He is our model. For we do not know, any more than he did, or to what extent *we* are being inspired by God in our hearts and motives and wills when we pray these inspired words; so we ask God to take His own inspired words more seriously than our own questionable meanings and motives.

David did the same thing at the end of another psalm (139) when, after hating and cursing his enemies and justifying this hatred with those stunningly self-satisfied words: "Do not I hate them, O LORD, that hate thee?... I hate them with perfect hatred", he added, "Search me, O God, and know my heart: try me, and know my thoughts. And see if there be any wicked way in me, and lead me in the way everlasting." If we sincerely add those words to all the other words we have spoken during life, we will go to Heaven. If we refuse to say that addition, we are in unspeakably great danger.

Psalm 27

"The LORD is my light and my salvation"

Each of the psalms I have selected has a unity, a single theme that is memorable and life-changing. In some, this theme reverberates throughout the verses (e.g., Psalms 1 and 23). In others, like Psalm 27, it is most memorable in a single verse. The point of Psalm 27 is its first verse.

> The LORD is my light and my salvation;
> whom shall I fear?
> the LORD is the strength of my life;
> of whom shall I be afraid?

The greatest thing is love. Love is a desire. The opposite of desire is fear. Therefore, as Saint John says, "there is no fear in love; but perfect love casteth out fear" (1 Jn 4:18).

In a sense, the whole of Christian education consists in learning what to love and what to fear. Here are two verses that tell us what to love and what to fear:

"Finally, brethren, whatsoever things are true, whatsoever things are honest, whatsoever things are just, whatsoever things are pure, whatsoever things are lovely, whatsoever things are of good report; if there be any virtue, and if there be any praise, think on these things" (Phil 4:8).

"And fear not them which kill the body, but are not able to kill the soul: but rather fear him which is able to destroy both soul and body in hell" (Mt 10:28).

Fear (repulsion) and desire (attraction) are the two most powerful forces in our lives. Each is the backside of the other.

Augustine says about love, which is the sum of all desires, "amor meus, pondus meum"—my love is my gravity, my weight, my destiny. I become what I love. I go where my love carries me: to unselfishness or selfishness, life or death, good or evil, Heaven or Hell, light or darkness, joy or misery, ultimately Christ or Antichrist. And fear is simply the backside of love. We fear only when we love. We fear to lose what we love.

We love many things, but God is the place where we find all of them: "light", "salvation", "strength", and "life" are four of the words the Psalmist uses here for what God is by His own essence and what He gives us as the properties of His grace, which is really His sharing with us some finite quantities of the infinite qualities of His own divine nature: "happiness", "blessedness", "truth", "goodness", "beauty", and "being" are a few of them. Any one of them can refer to all of them because in God they are always one; but with us, having any one of these does not necessarily mean having all the others (e.g., in us light may be in tension with life, or truth with power, or beauty with goodness). But if we have God, we have them all, for God is the "place" where they are all perfectly united.

And, therefore, when we have God, we have no need to fear the loss of any of them. "What shall I fear?" is a rhetorical question: the answer to that question is that there is no answer to that question, there is *nothing* we have to fear when we have God, because when we have God we have everything.

God designed our hearts to be like mirrors, reflecting all the light of the sun (which is an image of the Son—God is a punster). By the fall into sin, we have made ourselves twisted and broken mirrors. But we are still mirrors, not rocks. We cannot help but reflect the light, for that is what we essentially are: whether broken or unbroken mirrors, we are mirrors of divine goodness and truth and beauty. We cannot change our essential design, even though we can break it with our will and mistake it with our mind. We can break it or mistake it but not unmake it.

Of course, if this is not true, if there is no divine design, no sharing in divine life, divine grace, or divine gifts, then we can make ourselves into whatever we want: gods, clever apes, thinking vegetables, computers made of meat, angels trapped in material cages, transgendered contradictions, torture chambers, or devils. As the Paul Newman pro-suicide movie argued, *Whose Life Is It Anyway?* That is, indeed, the fundamental question.

The first two such gifts of God that the Psalmist mentions are "light" and "salvation". "Light" means "truth" or "correspondence to reality". "Salvation" means "eternal life" or "supernatural life" or "sharing in the very life of God", which life is love and joy. We need both of these two things, "light" (truth) and "salvation" (joy); for truth without joy is joyless truth and joy without truth is not true joy.

Light is the first thing mentioned because even though we can have light without salvation (we can know the truth but refuse it), we cannot have salvation without light. We can have the lights on in the operating room without getting the life-saving operation, but we cannot get the life-saving operation unless the lights are on. (The willingness to have the lights on is a main theme of both Psalm 139 and Psalm 51.)

So we all need light first of all, but how do we get it? Where do we find it? We can easily find knowledge, but where do we find wisdom? (See Job 28.) The answer is God. "In thy light shall we see light" (Ps 36:9). The "thy" is the most important word. All light is God's light. All truth is God's truth.

God *is* truth (which is naturally symbolized by light). He is neither subordinate nor superior to it. He is not subordinate or relative to any truth that transcends Him, and He is also not the arbitrary creator of a truth that is inferior to Him, that is a mere creature, like a platypus or a thunderstorm. God is truth. God is also love. That is why these are the two most absolute needs of man, who is made in the image and likeness of God. We might know some truth without knowing God, as we might see sunlight without seeing the sun on a cloudy day; but we cannot know God without knowing truth, just as we cannot see the sun without seeing sunlight, because God is "made of" truth, so to speak, as the sun is made of sunlight.

God is essential truth, substantial truth. The "Word" (*Logos*, one of the meanings of which is "truth") is "consubstantial" with the "I AM" who is the Father. That is why He can say "I AM the truth." John 14:6 refers back to John 1:1, just as John 1:1 refers back to Genesis 1:1. So also does 1 John 1:1. Compare and meditate on those three "beginning" verses.

And if we have this sunlight, this Sonlight—if we have Christ the *Logos*, the truth, the Mind of God—we have nothing to fear. Because that truth is also our salvation, our blessedness, our life. Job got truth when God appeared to him, and that was all he needed. Even before he got any of his stuff back, and even before his sores were healed and he got off his dung heap, he was satisfied. When you see God face to face, absolutely nothing else matters. God is everything. If He is not everything, He is not God. He gave Job his stuff back, but that was the icing, not the cake. In Heaven, when we see God face to face, we will also get everything else from God—friends, wisdom, contentment, joy—but even without those accidentals, those consequences, those gifts, we have everything because we have the essence, the cause, the Giver.

And we have Him *now*, if we are "in the Faith" and "in the state of grace", even though we do not see it or feel it as we will in Heaven. If you doubt that, read Romans 8:28–39. And remember, as you read it, that that is not a mere human opinion from a great saint (Paul). That is *God* speaking to you through His apostle. To *you*. It was designed for you, not for "human nature" or "humanity". God is not a company that addresses letters to "Dear occupant". He is your Father.

Thus the Psalmist says: I have God's light and life; therefore there is absolutely nothing left to fear. Light and life are everything we need. Even the disaster of Job's dung heap is trivial. Saint Teresa of Avila said that when we look back from the viewpoint of Heaven, the most horrible life on earth will appear no more serious than one night in an inconvenient hotel.

Christians have even more reason to pray this psalm. In Philippians 3:4–8, Saint Paul calls all his earthly righteousness, works, and perks to be *skubala* (the S-word in Greek; KJV dared to translate it literally as "dung"), compared with Christ: Roman citizenship, wisdom from the world's greatest rabbi, Gamaliel (Acts 22:3), and a life "which is in the law, blameless". What a liberatingly hilarious and hilariously liberating word that *skubala* can be! In the words of a simple song, "You can take every thing [on that big dung heap], just give me Jesus."

Once you know God, once you know who God is, once you know Him as your Everything and More-Than-Everything, you fear only one thing (losing God) because you love only one thing (getting God, which can only mean God getting you). Once you know who God is (the sum of all goodness and all joy), even two-thirds of the pains of Hell cease to be fearful, for "the pains of sense" and "the pains of regret" cannot add anything to "the pain of loss", the loss of God; for God is not the part but the whole. He is everything.

You would rather be with Him on the Cross than be with Pilate or Caesar in the richest and most comfortable palace in the world (see Ps 84:10). You would rather be Heaven's lowest slave than earth's highest king. Why? Because your Beloved is there. That is why you would rather be in love in the South Bronx than divorced in Hawaii.

In Purgatory, we will lack our earthly body and all the body's joys and needs and goods. We will also lack the peace and contentment of Heaven. In fact, Purgatory's greatest pain, according to mystics like Saint Catherine of Genoa, is precisely that lack, seen and felt with total clarity, without present comforts and illusions and diversions. Yet we will also have absolutely no fear because we will know that we are guaranteed eternal life; we will have God's infallible assurance of that.

Think of a man who is about to lose temporal life or the life of his beloved to a gunman. The gun jams, the bullet does not fire, and the gunman can only spit and shout and curse and glare at him. The man loses all fear. He laughs at the spitting and glaring. His temporal life has been saved. When our eternal life has been saved, we can laugh at the devil.

Here is the saint's secret of happiness: "Man, please thy Maker, and be merry / And set naught by this world a cherry" (William Dunbar).

When the wicked, even mine enemies and my
  foes, came upon me to eat up my flesh,
they stumbled and fell.
Though an host should encamp against me, my
  heart shall not fear:
though war should rise against me, in this will I
  be confident.

We do not know whether or not the Psalmist clearly knew
that our true enemies are not flesh and blood but principalities and powers of "wickedness in high places" (Eph
6:12). But both fall to the Son of David, as Goliath did
to David.

The inspired Hebrew Scriptures speak of our "enemies" hundreds of times, especially in the psalms. This is
not false, for life is war. That fact is not minimized but
maximized if our true enemies are not earthly but heavenly, not flesh and blood but "principalities and powers".
The physical wars are consequences, images, and appearances of the spiritual war, as the visible symptoms are
to the invisible disease. Wars on earth are always symptoms of the primal war in the heavens. We do really have
enemies, and they are far more formidable than human
tyrants, warriors, or giants. They want to eat us, destroy
us, body and soul, forever. If we saw them now clearly
and face to face, we would go insane with fear and panic.
But they shrivel at a single glance from the eyes of Christ
and grovel at His feet.

One thing have I desired of the LORD,
that will I seek after;
that I may dwell in the house of the LORD all the
  days of my life,
to behold the beauty of the LORD, and to enquire
  in his temple.

Why only "one thing"? Because God is only one thing. The wise and holy Psalmist's love and desire conform to the nature of reality. In other words, he is sane. Sanctity is simply sanity. Sanity is conformity to reality. In reality, God—the One God—is everything. In sanity, we love the One God with our one and whole heart. Like Saint Thomas Aquinas, who, alone in the chapel, hearing Christ's voice from the crucifix saying "You have written well of me, Thomas. What reward would you have for your labor?" replied: "Nothing but you, Lord." The most perfect possible answer!

That unity, that simplicity, is "the beauty of holiness" (Ps 29:2).

Our love and desire can be one and must become one because our God is one. Idolatry is the primal sin, the violation of the first and greatest commandment. Where do we see this violation? Polytheism is pretty much dead in theology today. But it is very much alive in our lives. What do we love most of the time, 23½ hours every day? Not God, but things, many things: consumer goods, pleasures, conveniences, relaxation, comforts, all examples of "my will be done." But the problem with "my will be done" is that my will is divided. If we are what we love, and if we love many things, we become many things, we lose the very image of God in us, the unifying power of personhood, the "I" of the "I am." That is what happens finally in Hell. You lose your soul, your self, your "I". And "what shall it profit a man, if he shall gain the whole world, and lose his own soul?" (Mk 8:36). That is what the worship of the one God saves us from.

We have not yet attained this unity, unless we are saints. Sin fractures it. Sin is separation from God *and therefore from ourselves*. As Thomas Merton says, "We are not at peace with others because we are not at peace with ourselves, and we are not at peace with ourselves because we are not at peace with God."

We must not only seek after a single God, but we must also seek after a single seeking, a pure motive. But seeking after a pure motive—seeking psychological unity—will not work unless it is subordinated to seeking after the one God. It is a byproduct, like happiness and health. Happiness addicts become unhappy, and health addicts (hypochondriacs) worry themselves sick. Similarly, eyeball-gazing seekers after psychic integration become disintegrated in their very search for integration. We must not center on "centering" but on God, who is the only true center and end. He cannot be used as a means to the end of our own centering. We must not seek seeking, center on centering, have faith in faith, hope in hope, or love love. We must seek, center on, trust, hope in, and love Him above all, with our whole heart; and only then will our heart be one.

That is what it means to dwell in the house of the Lord and behold His beauty. It is self-forgetful. That is what humility means: self-forgetfulness, not self-laceration; not a low image of yourself, but none; not putting yourself down, but not putting yourself anywhere except in His presence.

"The house of the LORD" is not simply our humility of heart. It is infinitely larger than us. God's house in Heaven will simply shatter all our poor imaginations and concepts, even the best ones. The great cathedrals of the Middle Ages were tiny appetizers of it. They were almost miraculous, vastly exceeding what could be expected from relatively primitive medieval technology. They stun, they humble, they convert, they bless. But there are no cathedrals in Heaven, because God's real "house" in Heaven is to the greatest and most miraculously wonderful cathedrals

on earth as those cathedrals are to a square foot of dirty
sidewalk in a slum. Heaven is to Notre Dame Cathedral
what Notre Dame is to Job's dung heap. If God's beauty is
not enough to keep us totally entranced for eternity, then
either we are not sane or God is not God. (Which of the
two do you think is more likely?)

> For in the time of trouble he shall hide me in his
>   pavilion:
> in the secret of his tabernacle shall he hide me;
> he shall set me up upon a rock.
> And now shall mine head be lifted up above mine
>   enemies round about me;

Meanwhile, it is not Heaven yet but Monday morning.
How does this Heavenly vision and hope change the
present life? This verse tells us. It does not keep us from
troubles, but it places them in a new place, a new context, which is here described by the military metaphor of a
"pavilion" and the liturgical image of a "tabernacle". We
are placed *inside* this new place, which is called both a fortress and a cathedral. It is, of course, the Church.

It looks very different from inside from what it looks
like from the outside. Anti-Catholics call this, derisively,
"organized religion". Catholics call it Noah's ark.

What is this faith that the Psalmist has in God? It is not
just a faith but a fact; it is not just a subjective attitude but
a truth. It is true because it "comes true" in history, in
time. Christ's coming is its verification, and His Second
Coming will be its second verification, which all will see.
His first coming is controversial and divisive: it leaves us
free to deny it or accept it. No one will be able to deny His
Second Coming any more than one can deny a tsunami.

Meanwhile, God lets us fall into "troubles" and wars,
with many "enemies", whether human (persecutors) or

subhuman (cancer cells) or superhuman (demons). We know that by reason and experience. What we do not know but can only believe is that God will always deliver us, hide us from destruction (though not from troubles), set us "up upon a rock", and put us in His "pavilion".

That is future: "he shall ... he shall ... he shall...." Only the future will prove this true, but the future *will* prove it true. It is very simple. You do not need to be a philosopher. Moses gave Israel the simplest possible test to distinguish false prophets from true prophets, false hopes from true hopes. The word is "wait". True prophecies and true hopes come true, false ones do not (Deut 18:22).

"Pavilion" is an old-fashioned word. Modern buildings that are "pavilions" are often impressive and strong public buildings, but in an earlier time a "pavilion" was usually just a large tent. Israel pitched its tents in the wilderness, un-pitched them, and moved on. It is an image for history, for time, and thus a good term to connote God's acts in time, culminating in the Incarnation. John probably had that image in mind when, in that incomparably profound poem with which he began his Gospel, he described the Incarnation in this way: "[he] dwelt among us" (Jn 1:14), that is, "he pitched his tent among us" (see Heb 8:2).

Just as a "pavilion" was just a large, public, open tent before it was a strong building, so the original "tabernacle" was a tent in the wilderness before it became Solomon's great temple in Jerusalem. Although of course the Psalmist did not know this, the ultimate meaning of the temporary "pavilion" tent in this psalm was to be the "tent" of temporal human "flesh" that the Eternal One "pitched" for thirty-three years of history and then rolled up and took to Heaven forever in his Ascension.

But a "pavilion" can also mean almost the opposite of a temporary, weak, mortal, flesh-like tent: it can also mean a strong, impregnable military fortress. That is perhaps the primary connotation the Psalmist means by the word here, for it is the first of four similar things he is listing as gifts God will give us if we hope in Him, four ways He will validate our trust. He promises (a) His pavilion, (b) His tabernacle, (c) a rock, and (d) victory. (That is what the lifting up of the head means; winners whoop, losers droop.)

All four images refer to the same thing: Christ.

(a) Luther had this kind of "pavilion" in mind when he wrote "A Mighty Fortress Is Our God." Christ is impregnable, unconquerable, mightier than even our most formidable spiritual enemies; Christ is stronger than Antichrist.

(b) Christ is present in the "tabernacles" on our altars and worshipped there.

(c) Christ is our "rock": "The Church's one foundation is Jesus Christ her Lord."

(d) And Christ is our "victory": He says, at the end of the Bible, "Behold, I make all things new" (Rev 21:5). That was not put at the end of the Bible because it was the end of the old order and the beginning of the new. The end happened at Calvary. That is why in *The Passion of the Christ* it was historically right for Mel Gibson to put those words into His mouth on the *via dolorosa*. Three hours later He said "It is finished" (Jn 19:30). The war has been won. The enemy has been defeated. The Incarnation was the invasion, and the invasion was successful. What remains is mop-up.

therefore will I offer in his tabernacle sacrifices of joy;
I will sing, yea, I will sing praises unto the LORD.

This (the previous verse) is such good news that the only response to it is song (this one). Now, even our sacrifices are "sacrifices of joy". To know Christ is to sing. Even old crows sing. If you do not sing, either you do not know Christ or you are severely repressed. So you need either an evangelist or a psychologist.

But you do not need singing lessons. The Psalmist never says "Make sophisticated and correct music to the Lord." He says: "Make a joyful noise unto God" (Ps 66:1). Even animals can make joyful noises. Are you less musically talented than an animal? Even my daughter's guinea pig makes squeaks of delight when she hugs her. Are you less able to sing than a guinea pig?

One of the main reasons Christianity is losing our culture (more accurately, our culture is losing Christianity) is that our religious life is typically many words but little music, much truth but little joy. You can argue with words; you cannot argue with music. You can argue with a saint's reasons; you cannot argue with his joy. It is irresistible.

Even in his prose, the Psalmist sings. He does not merely say "I *will* sing", he *does* sing. The word "yea" ("yes"—or rather "Yesssss!") in his last line is pure song. It does not add to the argument; it adds to the music. It means the same thing as "Amen!" We need a Black choir to teach us how to sing it right. If we do not know that singing, either we have missed Christ Himself or somehow missed His joy, or we are severely repressed, and our lips are not in tune with our hearts.

> Hear, O LORD, when I cry with my voice:
> have mercy also upon me, and answer me.

We are not sure whether these lines, and the rest of the psalm, were added from a different psalm, one whose spiritual mood was sorrow and weeping rather than joy, or whether these lines are to be interpreted in the context of the joy of the previous verse. In either case, it shows how closely joy is followed by sorrow and, therefore, also sorrow by joy. As Sinatra sings, "That's life."

> When thou saidst, Seek ye my face;
> my heart said unto thee,
> Thy face, LORD, will I seek.

The whole meaning of life is here. The meaning of life is to seek God. The meaning of life is not monologue but dialogue, not a private philosophy or mysticism but "religion", which means literally "relationship".

Our seeking God is neither the beginning nor the end. The end is finding God. The beginning is God seeking us. The beginning is God's revelation, God's interruption, God's barging in. The Bible begins with "In the beginning God ...", not "in the beginning I...." The first time any human writer in the Bible uses the word "I", it is God's speech (Ex 3:14), not his. The dialogue that is religion begins with God. True religion is not man's search for God but God's search for man. C. S. Lewis says that "agnostics will talk cheerfully about 'man's search for God.' To me ... they might as well have talked about the mouse's search for the cat." The wise old hymn says: "I sought the Lord and afterwards I knew / He moved my soul to seek Him, seeking me. / It was not I that found, O Savior true; / No, I was found by Thee." Augustine has God saying to him, "Take heart, my son: you would not be seeking me unless I had already found you."

The essence of atheism is not the failure to find God but the failure to seek Him. Atheism is not essentially the mind's opinion that God is nowhere to be found, but the will's free choice to say No to the divine invitation to seek Him that is inherent in our uncertainty and fallibility. For all who seek, find (Mt 7:7); thus to seek truly is to begin to cease being an atheist. No one loses Heaven by failing to find God, only by failing to seek Him.

What is it to seek Him? To seek is to be dissatisfied, to be uncomfortable. Comfortable atheists are in deep misery even though they do not feel it—precisely *because* they do not feel it. Happy atheists are not really happy, not blessed. Only unhappy atheists are. Atheists who seek, dissatisfied atheists, unhappy atheists, like Camus, are already responding with a Yes to God's invitation even though they have not yet found God. He promises that they will, that they will all find Him if only they seek: "he that seeketh findeth" (Mt 7:7–8). That is a solemn promise from God. I fear that many atheists who choose not to seek know all too well that they might someday find Him. That is what they are afraid of. I do not claim that this applies to all atheists, only some. But many atheists claim that it applies to none.

> Hide not thy face far from me;
> put not thy servant away in anger:

God is always there, but He often hides, for a variety of reasons. Only one of these reasons is His anger (at sin, of course, not at sinners: God practices what He preaches). His much more common reason is: to test our faith, to evoke more searching and longing and love on our part. A third reason is that if He revealed Himself fully, as He really is, to us in our present condition, we would dissolve like a gnat in a volcano.

The Psalmist fears God's anger. Of course, God cannot literally get angry, get carried away with a passion. But

God can say No, can judge, can punish; and that feels to us like anger, though it is in fact only justice and truth.

But God does hide, and we do not like that, though it is good for us. (He never does anything that is not good for us, because He does not have any "dark side" at all.) He truly hides (*vere latitas*) in the Eucharist, behind the appearances, like an actor in a costume. He hides behind nature, like an anonymous artist behind a masterpiece. He hides in our soul, and He does not give us the ecstasies and enlightenments that He could, though we long for them, for the same reason He does everything He does: because He loves us, and He sees that it is not good for us, not a cause of our greatest joy in the end, for us to develop a spiritual sweet tooth. So He gives us healthy vegetables instead of sugary candy.

God's "anger" is not literal, but it is real: it is His punishment, His justice; and we rightly fear that. Only a fool asks God for justice; the wise always ask for mercy. Our sins do not *deserve* mercy and forgiveness, so this verse's prayer is always appropriate for us. In the East, monks pray "the Jesus Prayer" constantly: "Lord Jesus Christ, Son of God, have mercy on me, a sinner." That prayer is our hope, and we should never lose hope; therefore, we should never lose that prayer, even in times of joy. For joy, too, is a mercy, not an entitlement.

> thou hast been my help;
> leave me not, neither forsake me, O God of my
>   salvation.

The Psalmist lets his past guide his future: God has always been his help in the past ("O God Our Help in Ages Past" is a great hymn title, as well as a great hymn), therefore he has good reason to hope for the future ("our hope for years to come"). There is empirical evidence, facts, history, behind his hope for the future. God *has* never forsaken him, therefore He *will* not ever forsake him. God has always been his help, therefore He will always be his help. This is not a desperate, fearful plea; it is a confident assurance of God's faithfulness: it is human fidelity responding to divine fidelity. ("Great Is Thy Faithfulness" is another great hymn title. The old hymns are nothing more or less than Scripture in song.) The Psalmist's petition is a petition for that which the Psalmist knows is divinely willed and therefore assured.

If it is assured, why then does he ask? He asks because God tells him to ask, with the promise that what he asks for will be given; but He wants us to ask for it. Asking for a gift is a free choice, just as much as giving a gift is. God's grace is a gift, and a gift must be not only freely given but also freely received. That is why "Please" and "Thank you" are two of the wisest things we can say.

And in the case of the gift of God's will, those two wise words ("please" and "thank you") can be identical. That seems impossible, since for us "please" comes before the gift and "thank you" comes after it. But God is not in time; for Him these two moments of the "before" and "after", the "please" and the "thank you", are not separated, as they are for us. And insofar as we say and mean "Thy (eternal) will be done", these two moments can be the same for us, too. And if not the same, at least joined indissolubly. Saint Thomas says that our will has two acts: to desire a good that is future and therefore presently absent to us, and to enjoy a good that is already present. To will God's will is to will both.

> When my father and my mother forsake me,
> then the LORD will take me up.

Did the Psalmist mean the first of these two lines as an impossibility, in comparison with which God's forsaking him would be even more impossible, or as a remote but real possibility with which he expected his readers to "identify" through their own experience, or through some friend's or acquaintance's experience, and which he was contrasting with the absolute impossibility of being forsaken by God? The point is the same either way about God. The only man God ever forsook (or seemed to) was His own Son; and that was only for three hours between noon and three; and that was for us, so that we could be adopted children of God and never be forsaken. He suffered our Hell so that we could be in His Heaven. The Great Exchange.

To be forsaken by your parents is even more traumatic and far more extreme than to be forsaken by the person you love the most, your spouse. In fact, half of all married people in America today are forsaken by their spouses. Husbands forsake wives as often as wives forsake husbands, but children forsake parents far more often than parents forsake children. For parents love children with a love that suffers for them, a love like God's. Children sometimes respond in kind, sometimes not. Jesus never calls God our Husband (though the prophets occasionally do: Is 54:5), but He always calls Him our Father. Jesus tells us how to think of God (He should know!): God is like the father of the Prodigal Son.

> Teach me thy way, O LORD,
> and lead me in a plain path,
> because of mine enemies.

Once is it established that God does not forsake us, the next step is that He actively leads us "in a plain path".

"Plain" means both (1) "simple and obvious" (Christianity is not hard because it is complex but because it is simple, far simpler than we are) and also (2) "straight" (not crooked) and "flat" (not treacherous from mountains or ravines). We need a straight path because we have enemies, we are at war, we are continually tempted and tried by the Enemy, and it would be terrible if we were tempted by God, too.

Of course, God does not tempt us. James explicitly says that (Jas 1:13–14). So when we pray "Lead us not into temptation", what should we mean by that? There are two possible answers. The first is simply that we mean "Do not allow the Enemy to tempt us." The second is to interpret "temptation", not as "egging us on to sin", but as "trials and tribulations that make our faith very difficult". So we are humbly confessing that our faith is weak and asking God to please temper His wind to us shorn lambs.

> Deliver me not over unto the will of mine enemies:
> for false witnesses are risen up against me,
> and such as breathe out cruelty.

God does not ever forsake us, but He does sometimes temporarily allow us to fail and fall and even to sin. When the Psalmist wrote "Deliver me not over unto the will of mine enemies", he probably meant only his military enemies. But we know there are far more serious spiritual enemies, Satan's minions, who are the "false witnesses" (liars) and accusers ("Satan" means "the accuser") who are "risen up against me", who "breathe out cruelty" because their very life ("breath") is hate. And so we naturally and rightly plead with Him to spare us that, as Christ Himself pleaded with Him in Gethsemane to, "if it be possible, let this cup pass from me" (Mt 26:39).

But even when He does apparently "deliver" us into the hands of our enemies, it is only temporary and for our eventual profit. All is part of the Plan. All things, including the physical evils that He allows us to suffer and even the spiritual and moral evils that He allows us to commit, if we repent and believe, become for us in the end part of the "all things" that He "work[s] together for good" (Rom 8:28). He makes no mistakes, and He "neither slumber[s] nor sleep[s]" (Ps 121:4). That is the God to whom we pray when we pray our most desperate prayers for help.

> I had fainted, unless I had believed to see
> the goodness of the LORD in the land of the living.

We do not need mere encouragement. We need much more than "try a little harder" or "Don't worry, be happy" or "Everything will be O.K." We need absolute assurance, a divine promise. Nothing less is the object of faith, as distinct from optimism. Without that faith, we "faint" dead away. No halfway measures will do.

Is "the land of the living" this world or the next? Both. Even here, all things, even evil things, are now working for our final good. And we can see this, though only "through a glass, darkly" and not "face to face" (1 Cor 13:12). But we can see enough to believe the rest. For what we see is Jesus (Heb 2:9). We see His Resurrection, and, therefore, we can believe in ours.

> Wait on the LORD: be of good courage,
> and he shall strengthen thine heart:
> wait, I say, on the LORD.

Courage is one of the most essential virtues. No one can endure this world without it. But we cannot achieve courage and spiritual strength all by ourselves. We cannot strengthen our own hearts with our own hearts or strengthen our wills with our own will, for you cannot give what you do not have. The leopard cannot change his own spots or the tiger his stripes. When we do succeed in maintaining and increasing our courage, that is always because God's grace is at work. But it does not work without our cooperation; what it perfects is our own free choices.

We "wait on" the Lord as a watchman waits for the morning (Is 21:12), not as waiters wait on customers in a restaurant. In fact, it is the opposite of the waiter in the restaurant: we "wait for" Him to come, and when He does, it is He who serves us. That was the shock the disciples felt when He washed their feet (Jn 13). When you see your Creator washing your feet and then dying for you, your pride falls down like Goliath or like the Tower of Babel, and your love flames up from the cold ashes in the hearth of your heart.

Psalm 42

"As the hart panteth after the water brooks"

> As the hart panteth after the water brooks,
> so panteth my soul after thee, O God.
> My soul thirsteth for God, for the living God:
> when shall I come and appear before God?

This psalm is memorable especially for a single word: the word "panteth" in the first line. It is memorable because it comes from the heart—indeed, from the heart of the heart—and it cuts to the heart. We bleed when we pray this.

It is not just desire or even love. It is longing. It is what C. S. Lewis made famous with the German word *Sehnsucht*. In the Romantic poets, it comes to eloquent expression, but it is in the deep heart of everyone, even if it is suppressed and unrecognized. The reason is that, as Augustine famously said, "Thou hast made us for Thyself and [therefore] our hearts are restless until they rest in Thee."

If our relation to God is not this "panting"—if it is anything milder and more comfortable than that—then we do not really know who God is. God is not just something; God is everything. If God is not everything, He is not anything.

If we understand this first verse, this "panting", then we will understand God; and if we understand God, we will understand Heaven; and if we understand Heaven, we will understand Hell, and we will understand why, when traditional Catholic theology speaks of the three aspects of Hell, namely, "the pain of loss (the loss of God, forever)", "the (bodily) pain of sense" ("fire"), and "the (spiritual) pain of regret and sorrow", we are more horrified by the first than by the other two. In fact, the first is sufficient; it is everything. If we understand God as He truly is, namely, as the One, the Only, the totality of good things to hope for and love, then we will understand that there can be nothing more to fear and nothing worse to fear than the loss of that one and only, that all. There can be nothing more in addition to the All to make Heaven better, and, for the same reason, there can be nothing worse than the loss of the All to make Hell worse.

In every desire, there is hidden a little bit of the desire for God. Desire for any good is a dim reflection of the desire for God, because any good is a dim reflection of the supreme and total Good, which is God. For there simply is in reality nothing else to desire. Whatever we find desirable in anything is a reflection of an attribute of God, whether it is a kind of truth or goodness or beauty. Christ's "I am the way, the truth, and the life" corresponds to these three values that we desire with our will, our mind, and our heart, the three powers of the soul that raise us above the animals and constitute the image of God in us.

Compared with the ultimately real, the Absolute, the little reflections of the real are almost nothing. In themselves, they are real; but compared with God, they are only shadows of the Real. Compared with God, the whole of creation, its highest "perks", are exactly what Saint Paul calls them in Philippians 3:8: "dung".

Our choice, in the end, is not between the one infinite good and many finite goods, not "God or politics" or

"God or sex" or "God or art", but, in the words of Cardinal Sarah's great title, *God or Nothing*. Hell is not just the absence of some goods; it is the absence of all.

Saint Augustine knew this zero-sum arithmetic of the soul. He said, "Whoever has God, has everything, and whoever has everything else but God has nothing, and whoever has God plus everything else does not have anything more than the one who has God alone."

The best way to understand this "panting" desire, and the reason the Psalmist compares it to the deer's matter-of-life-or-death thirst for water is to come near to dying thirst yourself—in your imagination, at least, if not literally. For to die is to lose everything. You *have* many things, but you *are* only one person, not many, and not a *thing*; and you have only one soul, and that is the source of life for every cell and organ and system in your body as well as the source of every desire and hope in your heart. To lose that, to lose your soul, is to lose everything. "For what shall it profit a man, if he shall gain the whole world, and lose his own soul?" (Mk 8:36). No one ever uttered a more practical principle of economics than that one.

This "panting" and "thirsting" for God is not, and cannot be, fully felt in our consciousness at every minute. That would be unendurable. Nor is it a single conscious choice, like a dramatic religious conversion, which Fundamentalists reduce to a clear, controllable thing. It is not essentially an emotion. Unemotional people and people who hide their emotions are just as capable of it as more emotional people and people who wear their hearts on their sleeves. Nor is it essentially a thought. It is not confined to "thinkers". It comes, not from the soul's conscious surface, of either intellect or emotions, but from the very deepest center of our being, from the heart of the heart. It is our "fundamental option", in Karl Rahner's terms. It determines our eternal destiny, for all get what they want.

That is why Jesus' very first question, in John's Gospel, is "What seek thee?" (Jn 1:38). For "he that seeketh findeth" (Mt 7:7–8). This is the terrible responsibility and glory of free will.

What does it mean to "thirst" for God? We cannot drink God; God is not water. We cannot use Him, as we use water; He is not a thing or a servant, a person who is treated like a thing to use.

Ah, but we *can* drink God. God *is* water. God is the real water, as He is the real food (Christ says, "my flesh is meat indeed"—Jn 6:55). The water we drink with our bodies is an image of the spiritual water that is the life (*zoe*) of God, not vice versa, for the body is an image of the soul, not vice versa. God is not like water; water is like Him. We die without water; we die without Him. Water is our life; He is our life. Water is our delight; He is our delight.

And as for serving us, He, our Lord and Master and God and Creator, does indeed serve us. He comes down to our world for us. He washes our feet, like a slave. He serves us the meal of His own flesh and blood on the Cross. And He continues that same meal in the Eucharist. He is the Host—*our* Host. We are His guests. In fact, when we drink His blood and live off it, we become His parasites.

The Psalmist knew nothing of this, of course: he did not know what he was thirsting for. Christ was what he was thirsting for. Christ alone, as perfect God and perfect man, not only reveals God to man but also reveals man to himself: Christ alone shows us what we most deeply and truly want. The thirst does not reveal what the water really is; the Water reveals what the thirst really is.

But what can we do with Him when we "get" Him? Nothing. But He can do something with us. He can do *all* things with us (Phil 4:13). The only thing we can do with Him is to love Him, to adore Him, to worship Him, to see Him and let ourselves be seen by Him, to "appear before" Him, as in Psalm 139. That is the Beatific Vision. This "vision" is two things, and the second is usually forgotten. It is not only our totally true and totally loving vision of God but also God's totally true and totally loving vision of us. The two visions meet and mingle, like the mutual gaze of two lovers. Thus Saint John says: "We know that, when he shall appear, we shall be like him; for we shall see him as he is" (1 Jn 3:2). We will see God as God sees us and, therefore, truly see ourselves, for we shall share in God's own vision. That is the water that alone can quench our deepest thirst. It is certain, complete, unending, unalloyed, unbreakable, unassailable, unimaginable, unspeakable, incomprehensible, indefinable, invulnerable, eternal, and ecstatic.

Do you really believe that your heart prefers money, sex, and power to *that*? Even if you will not listen to God speaking from on high, listen to Him speaking from below, from your own heart.

> My tears have been my meat day and night,
>   while they continually say unto me, Where is thy God?

Our "meat" (food) is what keeps us alive. In Heaven, that will be union with God Himself; in this life, it is the desire for God. The desire for God is not God—it is human, changeable, and fragile—but it has the shape (form) of God, so to speak, for it is not just desire but the desire *for God*, for the one, unique, and irreplaceable God. God has inscribed His own silhouette in our hearts. No smaller key will open that largest lock.

But we do not know God's essence or form (Jn 1:18), so how can we say it "has the shape of God, so to speak"?

Negatively. God can be known, and even defined. God is "that than which nothing greater can be thought". That is Saint Anselm's famous definition of God, and it is perfect, even if the "ontological argument" that he derives from the definition may not be a valid logical proof of God's existence. God is that which transcends all.

That is why we have a "lover's quarrel with the world". That is why this world is not enough: because that negative picture of God, that silhouette of God, that God-sized and God-shaped vacuum, that Grand Canyon in our soul, is so big that all the marbles in the world cannot begin to fill it. The whole universe cannot fill it.

But the part cannot be bigger than the whole, so how can our hearts be bigger than the universe of which they are parts? They cannot. Our physical heart is only a tiny part of the universe, but the spiritual heart of our soul is bigger than the universe. When the mindless giant that is the universe opens its gigantic, empty mouth to kill and eat you, you can say to it: I am bigger than you are, for even as your body swallows my body, my soul swallows your soul. The knower contains the known, not vice versa; and we know the universe, while the universe does not know us.

Our hearts are restless and "panting" because God designed them to be restless until they rest in Him. And therefore, until we are one with God, our soul's best food is the shape of God defined by His absence and our desire.

The panting is a great blessing because only those who seek, find; and those who pant, seek; therefore those who pant, find.

This panting is not just for super-saints and monks and mystics; it is for all the blessed. Next to God Himself, the greatest blessing in life is this panting.

This desire, this restlessness, this "panting", is even our souls' most *satisfying* food. This hunger is more precious than any other meal; this absence is more desirable than any other presence. For it is not nothingness; it is the absence *of God* and, thus, has the shape of God. That is why the great saints, like Mother Teresa, cherish even this apparent absence of God in their "dark night of the soul". It is not out of a Stoical duty alone. It is out of their love.

Who are the "they" who say continually "Where is thy God?" to the Psalmist? He probably meant the cynics who mocked his faith and hope, but we can easily allegorize them as the demons who originate this temptation to doubt and despair. "They" are also all anti-God temptations, including those that come, not from demons, but only from our own "world", i.e., our fallen culture and our own flesh, i.e., our own weakness and fallenness, the psychic forces in us that test and endanger our hopeful faith and faithful hope. For those psychic forces, though they are only human, are the spies and instruments of evil spirits. The War Room in Hell is full of brilliant strategists. Life is a constant struggle between faith and un-faith ("Lord, I believe; help thou mine unbelief"— Mk 9:24).

For only in a world in which faith is tempted and threatened and tested, only in a world where faith seems foolish, is faith even possible. In a world of constant miracles and mystical experiences (which is a world that God certainly *could* have created), there would be no room for faith. Only in a faithless world is faith possible.

Since "world" in Scripture usually means, not a space word, but a time word, that is, not the planet earth (*gaia*), but the culture of the times (*saecula*), the fallen world-order, therefore the shocking conclusion follows that only in a culture that repeats to us the taunts "Where is thy God?" can we choose to have faith. Faith cannot be an automatic given. It must have powerful alternatives.

Judaism appeared only in a Gentile and anti-Semitic world. Christianity flourishes the most where it is the most persecuted. In fact, only when faith is opposed by strong temptations and forces in its culture, only when faith is countercultural, can faith survive. Once the culture comfortably settles down to something taken for granted, once faith becomes culture, once faith becomes a useful and comfortable spiritual technology rather than a dangerous battle, the culture is doomed to apostasy and decadence, as we see today throughout contemporary Western civilization.

That does not mean we should pray for persecutions. But it does mean we should expect them. Nor does it mean we should not work to re-Christianize the culture. But it does mean we should "put no trust in princes". The culture, like the world, is to be neither despised nor idolized. We must be neither Fundamentalists nor Modernists.

> When I remember these things, I pour out my soul
>   in me:
> for I had gone with the multitude,
> I went with them to the house of God,
> with the voice of joy and praise,
> with a multitude that kept holyday.

Like the Psalmist, we long to turn back the clock to times when faith was popular and when that popularity was a joy. Such times are never allowed to remain for long in this world. If we try to live forever on the heights, we will fall. Only when our souls are "cast down" can they rise. Only when our hearts are broken can they be whole. Only when our stomachs are empty can God feed us. Only when we pant for God can God satisfy us. Only "by the rivers of Babylon", in exile, do we weep with longing for Jerusalem.

Diaspora is the norm, the to-be-expected situation, not the puzzling exception.

The past joys of the glory of the temple worship in Jerusalem for which the Psalmist nostalgically yearns are good, in fact God-approved, God-designed, and God-revealed; and it is natural to be nostalgic about them, as Catholics are about the glories of the Middle Ages, especially when compared with later exile or decadence. But they are like sweet treats. We appreciate them only by contrast. They are not our normal daily fare.

> Why art thou cast down, O my soul?
> and why art thou disquieted in me?
> hope thou in God:
> for I shall yet praise him for the help of his countenance.

The Psalmist now dialogues with his own soul. We can do that. Our deeper soul-level can speak to and instruct our shallower soul-level, as our adult self can speak to our childish self. For even though we are not yet spiritually adult but only children, we have an inner adult down there near the bottom of our childish heart. There is a wisdom and conscience that exists in the heart of even the shallow and selfish child. The same point can be made in reverse: there is a shallow and selfish child in even the mature adult.

The Psalmist now educates his soul. He tells his soul that it need not be "cast down" and "disquieted". We can be our own psychiatrist if we let God be ours first. We can talk wisely to ourselves if we first listen wisely to God. In fact, we know ourselves best when we forget ourselves and look to God. The more we focus on ourselves, the less we know ourselves. This is a paradox, an apparent contradiction. But it is true. No age has

ever been so self-focused, so psychological, so "addicted
to ingrown eyeballs", as ours; and the result is that we
understand ourselves much less clearly and certainly than
ever before in our history. My daughter, the psychologist, tells me there are at least thirteen different respect-
able schools of psychology in our culture, and they all
contradict each other somewhere.

The point is not that we should never try to "know
thyself" or examine our own conscience, but that we
should trust God more and ourselves less. We should
trust our egotistic self less but our deep self more when
our deep self tells us to turn our attention as well as our
trust toward God and not toward ourselves. The more
we "practice the presence of God", the more we get our
eyes away from mirrors (and iPhone screens and Face-
book!) and look at God (which is an utterly realistic
thing to do because He is really here!), the more we will
understand ourselves. The more we stop standing in our
own shadow, the more light we will see. That is "the
help of His countenance", the light of His face. When
we run from that light, we run into our own shadow
and disappear.

> O my God, my soul is cast down within me:
> therefore will I remember thee
> from the land of Jordan, and of the Hermonites,
> from the hill Mizar.

The Psalmist now turns from speaking to his own soul and
speaks to God. It would do no good to complain to his
own soul about the fact that it is "cast down within me".
God alone can heal it. And so he remembers the times
and places when God was closer, when his soul was not
"cast down" but full of joy in God and praise of God. And

he praises this God *now* and knows, by faith, that he still has this joy *now*, even though he does not feel it. For joy is more than a feeling: it is that which causes the feeling. That is God Himself.

The Psalmist speaks of "remembering" God, but this is not ordinary memory, like remembering a past thing or event or experience. God is not past, nor is He a thing, an event, or an experience. He is a Person.

Our present relationship to Him is both a remembering and a forgetting. In fact, it is a remembering of our forgetting, a consciousness of sin and alienation from Him, which is our true exile. Mental "forgetting" and moral "sinning" are not identical, but they are so closely related that each one is both a cause and an effect of the other.

Deep down, we all "remember" Him, even the unbeliever. That is why the unbeliever is guilty: he is responsible for what he knows, whether that knowledge is consciously admitted or not. Saint Paul says this very clearly in Romans 1: that there are none who do not "remember" God in two ways: externally and internally, nature and conscience. When we see nature, we see a great work of art, and art reveals the artist, as words reveal a speaker. We also know that we are morally responsible for being and doing good and not evil. Even if we do not clearly know the nature of the Artist or the nature of the Absolute Good, we know, "deep down", that there IS an Artist and an Absolute Good. That is enough to make us responsible, even if our theological beliefs about this Artist and this Good are uncertain, confused, or even idolatrous.

As a Jew, the Psalmist knows more than this "general revelation". He knows God's special, supernatural revelation through the Law (both the moral law and the liturgical laws God revealed to Moses), through prophets, and through the miracles of Jewish history. He has much to "remember" in his exile. We Gentiles are not in exile in

Babylon, as were the ancient Jews; but we are in exile in this post-Christian culture. And ever since a certain incident with a snake and an apple in a garden, we are all in exile "east of Eden". Therefore, what the Psalmist says about his exile is true for ours as well.

If our soul is *not* "cast down" like the Psalmist's soul by our exile, here "east of Eden"; if our exile from the Edenic relationship of God's presence does *not* depress us; then we are hopeless. Unbelief and atheism are not hopeless, but happy, contented unbelief and atheism are hopeless. A lost sheep is not hopeless, but a lost sheep that is satisfied with being lost and who is content with his exile as his only home is hopeless.

The second best thing in the world is to be in this depressed state of our souls being "cast down", because it is the prod that makes us seek, pant, and move toward the God and the Edenic relationship that we unconsciously and collectively remember. The only thing better than the agony of seeking is the joy of finding. The finding is Heaven, the agonized seeking is Purgatory, and the contented non-seeking is Hell. This life is either the beginning of Heaven (which is what Purgatory is) or the beginning of Hell. Unbelievers lack faith, but if they have hope, they may be saved, because hope leads to seeking, and seeking leads to finding. But if they lack hope as well, they have already passed under the sign on the door that announces: "Abandon all hope, ye who enter here." What door is that? Read Dante's *Inferno*.

> Deep calleth unto deep at the noise of thy waterspouts:
> all thy waves and thy billows are gone over me.

These matters are "deep" in two senses: they are both profound and mysterious, like the depths of the sea. The "deep" that "calls" is God; the "deep" that is called-to is the human heart, the "deep" part of the soul. The soul is like the sea: we see its clear surface all the time, but its unseen depths are far, far greater than its surface. The surface is only the surf-face. It is only skin deep.

The sea is also like our restless heart in that it is not always calm. In fact, it is never completely calm; even on windless days, it sighs and moves. Storms frequently arise on it, with "waterspouts" and great "waves and billows". They are wonderful yet terrifying. They are natural symbols of God's loving and warlike activity in our souls. When they involve suffering, they seem to be our enemy (they "are gone over me" apparently to drown me), yet they are a divine deep that "calleth" unto our human deep: they are a "good news", a hope, like a message in a bottle to castaways. The same divine ocean that exiles the castaways on an island far from inhabitable land produces waves that send them a "call", a message, a hope. The same God who is terrifying is also good—like Aslan. Incredibly, the same God who appears in fear, as "billows" and "waterspouts", is also a "song". That is the point of the next verse:

> Yet the LORD will command his lovingkindness in
>   the daytime,
> and in the night his song shall be with me,
> and my prayer unto the God of my life.

"Isn't life a terrible thing, thank God?" asks one of the characters in Dylan Thomas' *Under Milk Wood*. Like God, life is good news and bad news, fear and love, darkness and light, night and day. Thus the first word of this verse, "yet", summarizes everything. It is the contrast between appearance and reality, surface and depth, which is captured in the frequently used Greek idiom of *men* and

de, "on the one hand" and "on the other hand". That
is the essence of drama. It shows that life is not a formula but a story, and a story is interesting only because it
is surprising.

The great paradoxical secret is that this terrifying tornado
is a compassionate lover. God is not only love but lovingkindness; not only "tough love" but also tender love.

Love is a song: thus the title of the greatest love poem in
the world is "The Song of Songs", which means both "the
greatest song" and "the song that contains all songs". This
song is sung to us by God both in the night, when we do
not see Him, when only faith sustains us, and also in the
daytime, in what we do see. And therefore the Psalmist's
prayer arises from us, as it did from Christ, both in the
nighttime of the Cross, where it takes the form of "My
God, my God, why hast thou forsaken me?" (Mt 27:46).
And in the daytime of the Resurrection, where it takes
the form of Saint Thomas' "My LORD and my God!" (Jn
20:28). Both are prayers. Both are expressions of faith, for
Christ's "forsaken" prayer is still addressed to God. And
both are from the battlefield of doubt and temptation, for
Saint Thomas' confession addresses the very One he had
doubted. The daytime is still present in the night, through
memory and hope; and the night is still present in the daytime, through memory and repentance.

The Psalmist prays both night and day because his God
is "the God *of my life*", and life contains both night and
day, both "cast down" and resurrected, both "billows"
and "lovingkindness". In fact, the very "billows" are one
form that God's lovingkindness takes. The only reason
God lets us suffer "billows" is because He loves us. The
sun is still there even at night, even when the earth beneath
us eclipses it. Even "in the night his song [the love song]
shall be with me."

That does not make our night prayer into a day prayer. We still do not see during the night, and our prayer must be an honest and total confession of our experience, and therefore we still pray the next verse:

> I will say unto God my rock, Why hast thou forgotten me?
> why go I mourning because of the oppression of the enemy?
> As with a sword in my bones, mine enemies reproach me;
> while they say daily unto me, Where is thy God?

In other words, the "yet" works both ways. One way of putting it is that although God seems to abandon us, yet He does not. The other way of putting the same point is that although God does not abandon us, yet He seems to. Although the sun is not visible at night, yet it is still there; *and* although it is still there, yet it is not visible. Although love is a "song", yet we experience it as "mourning" and as "oppression" and as "a sword in my bones". *And* even though we experience God's love as hurt, yet it is "the wounded surgeon" who "plies the steel" (T. S. Eliot). Given our exile, our sin, such suffering is necessary; and so is our ignorance: we do not see the why of it. We see why suffering is necessary in general (we need surgery) but not in particular (why this, to me, now?). Why do we not see this? Because of who we are: we are not God. (It's a "Duh!", but God has to remind us of it, as He did to Job.)

In light of this truth of our non-divine identity and our consequent need for faith and hope, the Psalmist speaks to his own soul, reminding it of its need. His very soul is divided: the deeper part is God's prophet speaking out of the depths to the rest of it, encouraging faith and hope to the ripples on the surface, the ripples of feeling "cast down". What is really happening here in the inner drama of the Psalmist's soul is that Reason (in the old sense of wisdom, not the new sense of calculation and cleverness) is instructing and disciplining feeling, as all the premodern sages recommend and as the typically modern philosophers and psychologists say is impossible or unhealthy. The Psalmist reasons with his own soul and says:

> Why art thou cast down, O my soul?
> and why art thou disquieted within me?
> hope thou in God:
> for I shall yet praise him,
> who is the health of my countenance,
> and my God.

The thing his deepest heart pants for, like the hart thirsting for the water brooks, is nothing less than God. But God is here! He is truly present, even when we feel "cast down". He does not live in our feelings; He lives in our deep heart. He is not dependent on our feelings. He is just as really present when we are "disquieted" as when we are "quieted". Often, more so. The silhouette made by His absence to our feelings when we are "disquieted" is often sharper and more powerfully magnetic than the positive images that our happy feelings and imagination conjure up. Hope is responsible for that. Hope, like faith, is not a feeling. It is a *knowledge*.

Faith and hope always go together, for hope is simply faith in God's promises, faith directed toward the future. Faith is contrasted with sight, yet faith is a kind of sight, a knowing.

Present hope is not yet the future joy that is its fulfillment; yet hope is a kind of joy, already a fore-fulfillment, a foretaste or appetizer of the Heaven we hope for. Saint Catherine of Siena said that "All the way to Heaven is heaven." Even though we do not either feel or see the object of our faith and hope, who is God, nevertheless we know Him, we grasp Him, we meet Him, we touch Him, we *apprehend* Him (though we never *comprehend* Him) by faith and hope and, of course, by love. We do not know Him (*wissen, savoir*), but we do know Him (*kennen, connaître*).

But faith and hope and love are all free choices. That is why we have to keep doing what the Psalmist is doing here, namely, a holy talking and teaching and preaching to ourselves, instructing our own souls, reminding, remembering, remonstrating. We all have spiritual Attention Deficit Disorder. Even we who honestly and passionately profess the faith are absentminded professors. The Koran says the reason we need to pray five times a day is to get the rust of forgetfulness off our souls. That rust is what Muslims call *ghaflah*, a kind of innate "original forgetfulness" of the single most important truth, God Himself. The rust keeps accumulating, and unless we keep de-rusting our souls with prayer, eventually even the inner iron under the rust will rust away and dissolve.

That is what Hell is. Hell is all rust, no iron; Heaven is all iron, no rust. In Heaven, we will perfectly obey Saint Paul's command to "pray without ceasing" (1 Thess 5:17). (That does not mean "talk without ceasing", by the way; the most intimate prayer is silence.) We can fertilize and grow this "de-rusting" habit on earth by habitual prayer. It is our best preparation for Heaven.

It also gives us literally a happy face. That is the meaning of "the health of my countenance". A literal happy face, the face of a saint, is infinitely deeper—*thicker*—than the faces of the rich and famous and glamorous, which are thin masks, paper faces, that paper over an inner void. The paper face is two-dimensional: it lacks the deep wrinkles and twinkles of a Mother Teresa because it lacks the third dimension of depth, of soul, of *life*.

And of history, of the past. Your soul, right now, at this present moment, includes all of its past. Through memory, we preserve the past. Mere matter cannot transcend time like that. Memory is a kind of time-travel, not of the present into the past, but of the past into the present. Hope is also a kind of time-travel, of the future into the present. Only the soul has memory and hope, so only the soul can do time-travel. Your body does not pass through moments as a train passes through stations, leaving each one behind as it passes on to the next one. Rather, it rolls down the hill of time like a snowball, keeping the snow that it has accumulated from the beginning close to its heart.

The ultimate reason for the Psalmist's hope is in the little word "is". He hopes for deliverance and redemption and joy only because the God who gives it and who thus is "the health of my countenance" *is*. He is "my God" only because He *is* God, and not vice versa. Faith is not sight, but it is like sight in that both are "realistic", both correspond to reality, both are *true*. The only honest reason for anyone ever to believe anything is because it is true, because it really *is*.

Psalm 24

"Lift up your heads, O ye gates"

This psalm is more like music than words. It is a song—a song of triumph and rejoicing. Its first part praises God the transcendent Creator of the universe and asks who can ascend to His heights, beyond time and space and sin. The second part answers that question by praising the One who can do this impossible task. It is Christ, though He is not named except as "the King of Glory"; and He is on the march, triumphantly entering the gates of His kingdom. This could refer to

(a) His Incarnation, in which case the "gates" symbolize Mary; or

(b) His Resurrection, in which case the "gates" are the gates of death, which He shattered; or

(c) most obviously of all, His Ascension, in which case the gates are Heaven's gates and He is bringing to Heaven His "captives", His people, whom He has saved by His Incarnation, Passion, death, and Resurrection.

(I)

The earth is the LORD's, and the fulness thereof;
the world, and they that dwell therein.
For he hath founded it upon the seas,
and established it upon the floods.

The Psalmist first establishes the first fact, the fact of God and His ownership of all things on earth ("the fulness thereof"), especially mankind, "they that dwell therein", the only creatures that bear His image and that are loved for their own sake.

"The earth is the LORD's" because it is His signature. The most obvious argument for the existence of the Creator is the creation, just as the most obvious argument for the existence of the artist is his art. But the strongest argument *against* God is also the world: all the evil and suffering in it. As the ancient skeptic said, "If there is a God, how can we account for evil? But if there is no God, how can we account for good?"

This psalm is the definitive answer to evil because it is eschatological. It is a celebration of God's final, definitive triumph over evil. Evil's answer is given, not in an argument, but in a deed; not in timeless philosophy, but in an event. (The same is true of the problem of death: God's answer is not an explanation but a resurrection.) This event shows why God had allowed evil: only because out of it He would bring an even greater good.

> Who shall ascend into the hill of the LORD?
> or who shall stand in his holy place?

Yes, God is holy. But we are not. How can we possibly ascend into His presence and not die? How can the darkness endure the light? Only the holy can enter the holy place. The only answer to that question is Christ, who ascends as man and who *can* ascend because He is God. Man *needs* to ascend because he has descended, he has fallen, he is polluted. But man *cannot* "stand in his holy place". We are a living koan puzzle, a Catch-22.

He that hath clean hands,
and a pure heart;
who hath not lifted up his soul unto vanity,
nor sworn deceitfully.

This principle must be true. Dirt cannot pollute Heaven.
That would make Heaven un-Heavenly. But which of
us can say he is not polluted and unworthy? Life looks
embarrassingly like the classic Vermont farmer joke about
the lost New Yorker looking for directions: "You can't
get there from here."

He shall receive the blessing from the LORD,
and righteousness from the God of his salvation.

Justice demands these rewards, the rewards of righteousness, given to the righteous. But justice also forbids these
rewards coming to those who are not righteous. That
would be a lie. And God cannot lie. His justice is as absolute, as unavoidable, and as demanding as His mercy.

This is the generation of them that seek him,
that seek thy face, O Jacob. Selah.

Here is our unsolvable problem: we seek Him; we seek
His face; our deepest hearts demand nothing less than seeing God face to face. But no man can see God's face and
live (Ex 33:20) because no man is pure. The light of God
would dissolve us like the sun dissolving a cloud. We *must*
see God, yet we *cannot* see God.

We have no solution whatsoever to this greatest of all
problems. But God does. *Only* God does. There is no
human "way up" without a divine "way down". All other
religions are human ways up, and none work because
they don't get us to the very top. Christ is God's "way

down", and it "works" because it gets God to the very bottom. That is why there is no parity or equality among the world's religions, no matter how much great truth, goodness, and beauty they contain. There are many ways up, and no one of them can claim absolute superiority or exclusivity; but there is only one divine way down, only one man who is God.

(II)
Lift up your heads, O ye gates;
and be ye lift up, ye everlasting doors;
and the King of glory shall come in.

The "gates" or "doors" are "everlasting", so they must be the gates of Heaven. The Psalmist here addresses the gates of Heaven as if they were persons, with "heads", for he commands the gates to "lift up your heads." Perhaps they are angels, who man Heaven's gates and guard it against attacks from evil spirits as they guard us. The primary task of your guardian angel is defensive. Heaven sends us a personal defender against the tempting spirit from Hell who is more clever and powerful than we are, an angel who is the equal of a devil in power and cleverness, in order to preserve our freedom to cast the third and deciding vote in every moral choice we make.

These gates of Heaven are not raised except for those who belong in Heaven: Christ and Christians, the Lord and those who are His. Heaven's gates never rise to admit aliens and are never lowered against its rightful citizens.

Many who enter will be "anonymous Christians", those who through no fault of their own did not know that Christ was really the object of whatever faith, hope, and charity they had, that Christ was the One they were loving whenever they loved the good, and that Christ was the One they were obeying whenever they obeyed their conscience, His prophet in their souls. In the Last Judgment, He will claim all His own, and there will be many surprises for us, for we are not the Judge.

The King is "the King of glory" only because He has become the Man of Sorrows (Is 53:3). The Cross comes before the crown, for both Him and us. In fact, the marks of His greatest glory are the marks of His sorrow, namely, His wounds, which He carried even after His Resurrection. They are His badges of glory, as our lesser wounds will also be. His greatest glory is His humility—as ours will be also.

> Who is this king of glory?
> The LORD strong and mighty,
> the LORD mighty in battle.

The question is rhetorical. It is asked, not out of ignorance, but out of triumphant knowledge. The incarnate One has defeated all that Hell could hurl against Him: temptations, sorrows, sufferings in body and soul, hate, rejection, spitting, murder, crucifixion. The battle between Heaven and Hell began before man was created, and we were sucked and suckered into it at our beginning, in the Garden of Eden, and it will end only when time itself ends. The battle is life itself. The two truest images for life are love and war. Life is our romance with Heaven, and death is our romance with Hell. We come back, here at the end, to the beginning, to Psalm 1, to the two roads.

Although the two roads are equally open, the sides in the war are not equal, for the Lord is "mighty in battle". David, a thousand years before the Incarnation, is already celebrating God's victory.

> Lift up your heads, O ye gates;
> even lift them up, ye everlasting doors;
> and the King of glory shall come in.

Three whole lines are repeated word for word, like the chorus of a song. Repetition is the very structure of the psalms. The parallelism in each single verse is here reflected in the repetition of verses. It is like two blasts of a trumpet, rather than one: both an alpha and an omega (Rev 22:13). It is an expression in time of what is timeless.

This is why the Rosary is a perfect prayer: its three main components, the Our Father, the Hail Mary, and the Glory Be, are so perfect that no other prayer can rival them. Repetition chooses not to go out of them, out of the gates of their city, which is the City of God.

> Who is this king of glory?
> The LORD of hosts, he is the King of glory. Selah.

The rhetorical question "Who is this King of glory?" can be interpreted to mean: Who is this remarkable man Jesus? The answer is: He is God, He is "the LORD of [angel] hosts". The angels are *His* angels.

He is the King of glory in two senses: He is the King who eternally *has* glory, who wears glory like a garment, the One whose glory is reflected in all true glory; and He is also the King who redefines it, who transforms the meaning of glory from the vanity and pride of earthly Caesars into the love and self-giving service (the "foot-washing") that is the very life of God, so that to whatever extent we participate in that love, we participate in the glory of God. The very same glory that is in a cathedral is in a soup kitchen.

The word "Selah" is a liturgical term. No one but God now knows what it means. It is good that there are things like that, to remind us of our ignorance.

Psalm 137

"By the rivers of Babylon"

This is a mournful psalm, and a famous one, partly due to the short story by Stephen Vincent Benet, "By the Waters of Babylon". It expresses the sorrow of the Jews who are exiled and enslaved in Babylon. The ancients viewed exile far more seriously than we do, for they felt much more rooted to their home, their land, their nation for their very identity. Travel to foreign lands was a suffering, not an amusement or a holiday, for premodern peoples.

They also viewed slavery somewhat less seriously than we do, and as more normal for the same reason: they felt, not like autonomous individuals, as "free as a bird", but like members of a larger social organism, like leaves or branches on a tree. They preferred freedom (obviously), but did not absolutize it and idolize it, as we do.

The psalm also expresses the Jews' love for Jerusalem and its great temple of Solomon, or rather of God, for it was invented and commanded by God Himself, in detail (see 2 Chron 2–8).

The two themes of sorrow and love are closely connected, for nothing shows one's love for a person, place, or thing as much as the suffering of being separated from the beloved. And in this case, the beloved is all three, for the Jews' connection with Jerusalem (the place) and the temple (the thing) and Sabbath worship (the time) was a connection with the Person of God. That is what it means to be a "holy" place (Jerusalem) or thing (the Temple) or time (the Sabbath).

> By the rivers of Babylon, there we sat down,
> yea, we wept, when we remembered Zion.

Memory is a strange thing: it makes us look at past joys with sorrow and past sorrows with joy. It increases sorrow when what is remembered are joys that are past and cannot be recaptured; and it increases joy when what is remembered are pains that are over and no longer feared. Thus, not only did the memory of the past joys of the temple increase the sorrow of the exiles, but the return from exile increased their joy by contrast to the remembered sorrow of the exile.

> We hanged our harps upon the willows in the
>   midst thereof.
> For there they that carried us away captive required
>   of us a song;
> and they that wasted us required of us mirth,
> saying, Sing us one of the songs of Zion.
> How shall we sing the LORD's song in a strange land?
> If I forget thee, O Jerusalem, let my right hand
>   forget her cunning.
> If I do not remember thee, let my tongue cleave to
>   the roof of my mouth;
> if I prefer not Jerusalem above my chief joy.

Picture the scene. Notice every word. It is utterly concrete, both within and without. It is quite literal. No additional words are necessary or even useful.

The reason for this tremendous sorrow is not merely that the Jews were enslaved. It was something worse than slavery: it was exile; it was homelessness. And it was even worse than the homelessness that any other ancients felt when they were exiled from their native land. The Jews were exiled from the Holy City, Jerusalem. Jerusalem contained Solomon's temple, the place where heaven and earth met, the place where God's will was done, the place where sacrifice was made. And sacrifice was essential to religion for all the ancients. We moderns have forgotten it, even despised it as "primitive" or "repressive", or limited it to something merely subjective and psychological. Imagine a pious Catholic never again being allowed to enter a church, hear Mass, or receive a sacrament. Imagine a quarantine from a pandemic that lasts a lifetime.

It was only the Jews' piety and love of their God and their worship and their temple and their city that was responsible for their suffering. For the more you love, the more you can suffer.

Now comes the shock:

> Remember, O LORD, the children of Edom in the
>   day of Jerusalem;
> who said, Rase it, rase it, even to the foundation
>   thereof.
> O daughter of Babylon, who art to be destroyed;
> happy shall he be, that rewardeth thee as thou hast
>   served us.
> Happy shall he be, that taketh and dasheth thy little
>   ones against the stones.

What is most shocking is the timing here. It is immediately after the previous expressions of tender, sensitive, sorrowing, loving piety that we find something that it is almost impossible to believe came from the same heart of the same Psalmist at almost the same moment: undisguised, murderous hate, raging, fiery, adamant, and volcanic.

Ironically, after laying a conditional curse on his own right hand and tongue, in the previous verse, if they failed to participate in his sorrow, he now curses, in a totally non-ironic and unconditional way, the people responsible for that exile, right down to their innocent little babies, and blesses those who murder them. Let us not try to soften it. The last two lines of the passage say nothing less than this: "I bless, and I call God to bless, anyone who seizes a little innocent Babylonian baby and smashes his skull against a rock, scattering his brains on the ground."

No Christian, no pious Jew, no religious person at all, no morally sane atheist or agnostic, can speak these lines, in prayer or in thought, without radically reinterpreting their overt meaning. The only way we can use these curses is to turn them upside down and backward, to make them even more ironic than the Psalmist's cursing of his own right hand and tongue.

We have a model for this. This is also how we must interpret, and how we must believe God interpreted, the Jews' self-cursing at the trial of Christ when they said, "His blood be on us, and on our children" (Mt 27:25). God did indeed let His Son's blood be upon them and their children, but to save them, not to damn them! And not just them, but the whole world. That was symbolized by the fact that the curse, the condemnation, the charge against Christ was written, on the Cross, in all three of the world's most important languages, Hebrew and Greek and Latin (Jn 19:20). All of us crucified Christ by our sins. And all of us were included in Christ's prayer from the Cross to forgive the very sinners who crucified Him. He shed all His blood for all those who shed His blood. He turned a Passion into an action, a murder into a Resurrection, the greatest evil that ever happened into the greatest good that ever happened, which Christians celebrate on a holy day that they dare to call "Good Friday".

Saint Benedict shows us how to pray these verses. We must allegorize them. Babylon is a symbol for Hell's kingdom. This is what must be done with the word "enemies", which occurs hundreds of times in the psalms, usually in cursings. The physical, flesh and blood enemies (the Babylonians) are symbols for our real enemies, which, as Saint Paul has told us (Eph 6:12), are not flesh and blood but "principalities" and "powers" and "spiritual wickedness in high places". They are demons, evil spirits, including those that tempt us. And what are these demons' most powerful weapons? They are our own sins, which we are indeed obligated to hate and fear far more than we do. And the Babylonian babies are baby *thoughts*, which are the first source of every sin, as they were for Eve in the Garden. We must have absolutely no pity or compassion or sympathy or tolerance for them. We must do to them exactly what Christ did to the serpent as soon as he saw it in that other garden, Gethsemane, in the very first scene of *The Passion of the Christ*. We must instantly stomp on it to smash its brains out, that is, its mind, its tempting thoughts. For we must bring "into captivity every thought to the obedience of Christ" (2 Cor 10:5), because all sin and all virtue begin with thought. Giving your thoughts to God is like giving your babies to God.

What does God think about the Psalmist's cursing prayers? God answers all prayers, but often His answer is No. This applies to our curses as well as to our blessings. God clearly did not take the Psalmist's prayer literally, accept it, and bless flesh-and-blood Babylonian-baby-killers; just as He did not take literally and accept the self-curse of the Jewish (and Roman) Christ-killers.

This raises the troubling theological question of the divine "wrath" (hate). Scripture frequently affirms the reality of "the wrath of God". It also affirms that we are to be Godlike. "You must be holy, as I the Lord your God am holy" is a repeated formula in Leviticus—e.g., 20:26. Yet we are to love and not to hate. There seems to be a logical self-contradiction in affirming all three of these oft-repeated scriptural commands.

God's anger differs from ours in three ways. First, it is always just and right and righteous and true. Second, it is not a changing emotion, a fit of feeling. We cannot wait for Him to "get over it". It is necessary and eternal. Third, most important of all, its object is not sinners but sins. As ours should also be. "Hate the sin, love the sinner" because the whole reason for hating the sin is love for the sinner, as the whole reason for a surgeon hating the cancer is love for the patient. And God preaches only what He practices. We are to be holy *as He is holy* (Lev 11:44). And that is exactly how He is holy: He is holy both by loving sinners and by hating sins *because* He loves sinners and sin is their real enemy.

One of the ways we differ from the saints is that we have far too little passion, anger, hate, and wrath against sins, especially our own. Every sin must suffer its just punishment. It is condemned to death, eternal death. If we repent of our sins, if we dissolve the glue between our will and our sins, we do not go with them to the place of eternal death. If we do not love our spiritual garbage, we do not go with it to the garbage dump. But if we do love our sins, if we glue our heart to them and do not repent of them, if our sins constitute our chosen identity, then we must share their fate, and the Bible's name for that fate is Gehenna.

"Gehenna", Jesus' name for Hell, was a large garbage pit in a valley outside Jerusalem. In it, garbage was burned to ashes continually, day and night. (It was hard to re-light fires in an age without matches.) Nothing living could survive that fire. Hell is never described in the Bible as a place of eternal life, even life with pain, but as one of eternal death. Death is worse than pain, because "while there's life, there's hope", but the words over Hell's entrance are: "Abandon all hope, ye who enter here." (Dante got it right.)

This brings up the question of how we who believe that "God is love" (1 Jn 4:16) can believe in the reality of Hell. Of all the many truths God has revealed to us, that is the one we find, or at least ought to find, the hardest to accept, if we understand who God really is. God is love, and Hell is hate, and the two are opposites, and if one of two opposites is infinite, there seems to be no room left in reality for the other one. Yet Jesus, love incarnate and the most compassionate and forgiving and merciful man who ever lived, clearly taught the existence of Hell. What do we do about this?

One thing we should not do, or dare to do, is to be so arrogant as to patronize Him and gently correct Him and pity Him for not sharing our modern sensitivities or for not being intelligent enough to see our logic. How dare we think that we know better than He does about such things? Like good scientists, we must accept and reconcile all our data, not just prefer some and ignore others.

Jesus came to save us, to loose us from our spiritual garbage, from our sins—all of them. Why, then, is there a Hell? Because salvation is a gift, and a gift must be freely accepted. We cannot "do" salvation without Him, but He will not do it without us, without our free consent. It is the Godfather who "makes you an offer that you can't refuse". God the Father makes you an offer that you can.

The only defense of Hell, the only reason for it, the only real cause of its existence, is human free will. Look hard at the doctrine of free will, and you find the doctrine

of Hell as a necessary consequence of it. It is logically inescapable. If salvation must be freely chosen, well, then it
must be freely chosen, not compelled or imposed. And
that means it can be refused.

After a similar prayer of cursing in Psalm 139:19–22,
the Psalmist added vv. 23–24: "Search me, O God, and
know my heart: try me, and know my thoughts: And see
if there be any wicked way in me, and lead me in the way
everlasting." We can only hope that he prayed the same
crucial postscript here.

Psalm 96

"O sing unto the LORD a new song"

Religion is a *song*, not a formula. But it seems to be an *old* song, a song of timeless, unchanging things, and therefore "traditional", not "progressive". The pessimistic philosopher wrote "There is nothing new under the sun" (Eccl 1:9).

He was wrong.

God is new, always new, never old, never boring, never predictable. And God acts "under the sun", in time. Judaism is the history of God acting in time. Judaism was the only religion in the ancient world with such a God, a *real* one. The test of reality, as distinct from fantasy or ideology or idealization, is action. Only real beings can act. Thoughts cannot.

The "new song" is the "good news", the Gospel. It is not called the "good olds". It is the newest thing that ever happened. It is the most astonishing event of all time, the event Kierkegaard called "the absolute paradox": that which had no beginning had a beginning: the eternal God entered time as a human being. The eternal Creator of the sun was literally "under the sun", the astronomical marker of time, for thirty-three revolutions of the earth around the sun. The eternal Logos became flesh (Jn 1:14). Divine Truth became a member of our species. Saint John in his old age cannot help marveling at this: "That which was from the beginning, which we have heard, which we have seen with our eyes, which we have looked upon, and our hands have handled [is] ... the Word of life [the *logos* of *zoe*]; For the life was manifested, and we have seen it" (1 Jn 1:1–2). The "new song" is Christ.

> sing unto the LORD, all the earth.

The Psalmist is humbled before God, and therefore he realizes that his singing is radically inadequate. So is that of the whole human race. The main reason it is inadequate is that it is polluted, it is fallen, it is full of sin as well as holiness. He therefore calls upon the whole earth, the whole of creation, which is sinless, to sing this "praise chorus". This is the real "praise chorus", and it is infinitely more beautiful and profound than our well-intentioned but embarrassingly shallow and childish efforts by that name.

Later in this psalm (vv. 11–12) he is even more specific about the identity of the singers:

> Let the heavens rejoice, and let the earth be glad;
> let the sea roar, and the fulness thereof.
> Let the field be joyful, and all that is therein:
> then shall all the trees of the wood rejoice

Inanimate things cannot rejoice, be glad, roar, or be joyful, so this must be a clever personification, a mere metaphor, not a reality, except in the poet's mind and will, right? He is imagining them doing this, he is wishing them to do it, he is telling them to do it, but they are not really doing it, right? Wrong. It is real. The heavens and the earth, the sea and the field, and all the trees are being called upon to do *what they in fact are doing*: praising God, glorifying God, sharing His joy with us, as a love letter really does actively share the love of its writer with its reader even though ink and paper are not animate. The trees are really rejoicing. In fact, they are really clapping their hands (Is 55:12). They are clapping their hands even though their hands are not made of flesh and bone, and they are rejoicing even though they do not have rational souls that can understand and choose to rejoice. For they are participating in the Psalmist's rejoicing, as a sword participates in a warrior's fighting, as a love letter participates in the lover's love, and as the cymbals the musician uses are participating in the music he is making. They are praising the Lord. They are doing it on a lower level of the great chain of being, the cosmic hierarchy, than man, but they are doing it. And man is raising them up to his level and enabling them to participate in human rational, moral, and religious acts even though they are not themselves rational, moral, or religious agents. For man is the cosmic priest, and his offering is the entire cosmos. It is sacramental. The whole universe is a sacrament, and it is singing.

> Sing unto the LORD, bless his name;
> shew forth his salvation from day to day.

The whole universe is doing it, is singing to God, praising God, blessing and glorifying His name, so how dare we stand aside from this song?

The Psalmist encourages us to sing "unto" the Lord, not just *about* Him. The song is a prayer.

What is it to "bless his name"? To "bless" is not necessarily to give some gift that will improve the recipient. No one can do that to God. But to "bless" can also mean simply to praise and rejoice in and sing about the blessings, the perfections, that He already has in infinite supply.

And his "name" is not merely the word in our language that refers to Him, it is He Himself. "In the name of" means "in the real power and presence and authority of", like a signature on a check or a soldier executing his commanding officer's order.

("Authority", by the way, is usually misunderstood today. It is neither mere force, executed with irresistible necessity, nor mere example, offered for free imitation, but something between the two.) We are neither forced nor merely invited, but authoritatively exhorted to sing and bless and praise God.

We are even exhorted to *thank* Him simply for being what He is, quite apart from any gifts He gives to us. The Gloria sings: "We give you thanks for your great glory." Even if He gave us none of His gifts, He deserves thanks and gratitude for being what He is because that fact, once known, blesses us and increases our joy and appreciation. Just to know that a great person, a great act, a great work of art, or a beautiful place exists is enough to give us joy and comfort. The symphony or the statue or the star does not deliberately choose to give us joy, but it does, simply by being what it is. How much more must God give us joy not only by what He does but also by what He is.

Here is a test of whether you appreciate this point. It is important because it gets us out of our reigning subjectivism and egotism. C. S. Lewis, in his autobiography, *Surprised by Joy*, discovered it one day, to his surprise, when he realized that "it is more important that Heaven should exist than that any of us should reach it." I hope something in you understands that.

But we not only know that Heaven exists but also that we can go there, to that place that is so beautiful that its sheer existence is more important than our experience of it; and we are invited to praise God not only for what He

is but also for what He has done for us, which is His gift of
what He is, of Himself.

Notice that the word here is "praise", not just "thank"
(though of course it is that, too). Appreciation (and, in
the case of God, adoration) is even more than gratitude
and thanksgiving for His gifts, because what God *is* is
even more than what He *does*. Dmitri Karamazov says
to God that even if He sends him to Hell he will praise
Him there, "from the underground". Even if a distant
galaxy does not shine upon us, even if a great work of
art is never seen or heard by us, its beauty and glory are
worthy of our praise.

> Declare his glory among the heathen,
> his wonders among all people.

Even a thousand years before the Christian and missionary
era, the Psalmist knew that this unique Jewish revelation
is to be preached to "all people", especially to those who
have not heard it, whether this not having heard it is due
to their own fault or not. It is also to be preached to those
who have heard it and disbelieved it through their own
cynicism or dis-appreciated it through their own hardness
of heart. It is also to be preached to those who do believe
it, to remind them (for we all have serious spiritual memory loss). We all know people in all three of the above
classes. Indeed, we ourselves, with at least parts of ourselves, frequently migrate into and out of all three of the
above classes.

> For the LORD is great, and greatly to be praised:
> he is to be feared above all gods.
> For all the gods of the nations are idols;
> But the LORD made the heavens.

In a sense, there are no atheists: everyone has some God, some First Thing, some Greatest Good. Perhaps there are as many of them as there are people on earth, since the first god we worship, coming out of the womb, is ourselves.

The Psalmist here paints with a very broad brush: all gods except God are idols, all candidates for the one "to be feared above all" are false except one. When you compare these many different idols to each other, such a broad condemnation seems irrationally narrow, but when you compare them to the true God, it appears absolutely necessary. Those who complain about the religion of the Bible being narrow and judgmental reveal nothing about the Bible but much about themselves: they show that they have never understood and appreciated the true God. He is to all other gods as the sun is to matches or as Antarctica is to a single snowflake. For He alone "made the heavens" (i.e., the universe) and, therefore, all the things in it that we have worshipped as our idols, including ourselves.

> Honour and majesty are before him:
> strength and beauty are in his sanctuary.

These four divine attributes of honor, majesty, strength, and beauty (these four stand for *all* of the divine attributes) are conceived here as if they were soldiers or servants standing "before him" and "in his sanctuary". They are relative to Him, not He to them. We do not worship God only because He conforms to the Platonic Idea of the Good; we worship the Platonic Idea of the Good only because it is an attribute of God. We worship a "Him", not an "It". We worship the Divine Persons, not the divine nature. We may admire and contemplate the divine attributes (the ones that we understand a little bit, at any rate), but we do not worship them; we worship the God who possesses them.

They are His attributes, He is not theirs. Religion is an I-Thou relationship, not an I-It relationship.

> Give unto the LORD, O ye kindreds of the people,
> give unto the LORD glory and strength.
> Give unto the LORD the glory due unto his name:

When we praise God, we do not, of course, "give" Him anything that increases or changes Him, but, in forgetting ourselves in praising Him, we give ourselves something that changes us. We increase our wisdom (for every wise action increases the habit of wisdom from which it proceeds, as a kind of feedback) and our righteousness, or justice (for the same reason), and our joy (for wisdom in the reason and righteousness in the moral will are the two chief causes of joy in the heart).

> bring an offering, and come into his courts.

How do we "give unto the Lord"? How do we translate this general and abstract act into a concrete one? The most concrete way is by going to church, by moving our bodies into a different place, a holy place, and by bringing an "offering" there. The "offering" is ourselves, our presence, our bodily presence, first of all.

And, of course, our mind and will and heart, the three powers of our soul; for our soul is wherever our body is. Then, perhaps we offer also money or, if we were ancient Jews, an animal. But whatever material thing we offer, including our own bodies, it is offered by our soul and also along with our soul (for the soul can offer itself). The heart of the soul is the heart of the offering. Everything else we offer is offered by our heart, our will, our choice, our love, our soul's captain.

O worship the LORD in the beauty of holiness:

Because holiness is beautiful, beauty is holy. "The beauty of holiness" does not mean the aesthetic virtues of the architectural qualities of the church building but the moral virtues of the persons who are the church's "members" (which for Saint Paul, in 1 Corinthians 12:12–30, are organs, as in a body). Their holiness, their sanctity, is the most beautiful thing in the world. That is why Mother Teresa's wrinkled face is more beautiful than the Mona Lisa and why Christ's bloody wounds are more beautiful than Hercules' mighty muscles. The beauty of a great cathedral is great only because it is made by and expresses the beauty of the holiness of the souls of its designers.

fear before him, all the earth.

Whenever we are commanded to "fear" God, it is filial fear, not servile fear, that is commanded. For God is a Father, not a slave-master, and we are to fear displeasing our Father, not our tyrant. "Fear" also means awe, wonder, and worship. If we do not begin there, then all our talk about God's love and mercy and compassion becomes cheap and cuddly. Most Muslims begin there and fail to proceed to love; most Christians fail to begin there and proceed to confuse love with "luv". God's Son did indeed become a lamb, but this is amazing only because He is first the Lion.

Say among the heathen that the LORD reigneth:

We are commanded to speak of the true God "among the heathen" because the whole earth is commanded to "fear before him". The justification for this mission, this missionary work, is cosmic. If there are other intelligent races on other planets, they, too, are creatures of the same God. Perhaps they know Him in ways we do not, so we could be missionaries to each other. To a certain extent, and with important qualifications, perhaps that is true even of the different religions of this world. Vatican Council II encouraged us to learn from other religions, for all truth is God's truth, and truth can never contradict truth.

> the world also shall be established that it shall not
>   be moved:

I am not sure why this line is here. Probably, the stability of the earth was more impressive, as an example of God's eternity and greatness, to the Psalmist than it is to us, for we know the relativity and the fragility of all apparent stability anywhere in the physical universe more than pre-Einstein peoples did.

> he shall judge the people righteously....
> For he cometh to judge the earth:
> he shall judge the world with righteousness,
>   and the people with his truth.

In three ways, He comes three times. The first way is the revelation of the Father, in the Old Testament, of the Son, in the Gospels, and of the Holy Spirit, in the Church. The second way is the three comings of the Son: in Bethlehem in the past, into our lives in the present, and into the world at the second coming, the Last Judgment. The third set of three comings are the three "books" or revelations of God: in nature, to His "chosen people" the Jews, and in Christ.

Let us look at this third set of three comings for a moment. The creation is the first of God's three love letters to us. It is the letter written in material things—all things. The second letter is written in miraculous deeds and inspired words, which are collected in a Book. We are studying parts of that Book in this book. The third and supreme one is written in human flesh, especially when that flesh is nailed to the wood of the Cross.

The third coming is the supreme one. The practical "payoff", or "existential" bite, of our faith in God is the future. The fruit of faith is hope. Faith is the seed, and hope is the plant.

God is, timelessly, and therefore He is both the most ancient and absolute foundation and beginning, the most ubiquitous presence in the present, and the guarantee of a perfection of joy and justice in the future. He "cometh" implies all three: that He came in the past with His "mighty deeds" and "strong right hand", that He comes in the present to meet and lovingly confront and interfere with and radically change our lives, and that He will come in the future to complete our salvation and sanctification.

And because this future's quality is immeasurably great, and the quantity of time between now and then is immeasurably short, He can truly say, in His very last words in Scripture, that He will come "quickly" (Rev 22:20). For quantity is relative to quality.

His threefold coming to us, from past and present and future, is unlike the coming of any thing or event that is in time and that is limited by time. Time separates the present from both the past and the future and separates the past from the future; eternity unites them. That is why God, who is not limited by time, comes to us out of all three dimensions of time.

He comes to us out of our past, not just in our memory but really: He resurrects the past and makes it live for us, makes it really present. (The dying who see their whole past life pass before them often say that it was not just observing it but living it and feeling it as present.)

He comes to us in the present, both in the timeless "now" that takes no time at all and in the "now" that includes the flowing present that extends vaguely, without clear limit, into the very recent past and the very closely anticipated future.

He comes to us even out of the future, for He is already there, as we are not. He bilocates not only in space (His ubiquity or omnipresence) but also in time. He is every-when as well as everywhere.

He will come to "judge". That "judgment" is not the opposite of "salvation" but identical with it for the blessed, but not for the damned. For "judgment" means essentially "truth", and truth is what will equally, at the same time and for the same reason, bless the blessed and also damn the damned.

This sounds paradoxical, but it is easy to explain how it works. The same mercy is extended to all; the blessed accept it, in humility and repentance and faith; the damned do not. The result is judgment and justice for both. The same light shows up both as they are. No force is used on either, but our own freedom and free will and free choice determine our destiny, for they determine our relationship to that light, that Truth. (That is the point of both Psalm 1 and Psalm 139.) So ultimately, these four things, mercy and justice and truth and freedom, are identical.

Psalm 150

"Praise ye the LORD"

This psalm is almost as short as the first, for like the first it has only one point. That point is very clear and obvious, and it is the most repeated command in all 150 of the psalms. It is put in the very first line:

Praise ye the LORD.

All other right attitudes to God can be and should be incorporated into and colored by praise. That includes complaining, questioning, petitioning, repenting, and thanking. If any of these are devoid of praise, they are incomplete.

※

Why are the psalms full of "praising"? Why does God want our praises? Is He a despot with an ego that needs stroking? Does He lack self-esteem? Does He need confirmation of His goodness? Is He insecure in His power? Does He want to reduce us to sniveling slaves? When a human being demands praise from his fellowmen, that is what we rightly suspect. But we are not God's fellow gods (Stop the presses! Call the reporters!), nor is He our fellow creature. Both His demand for praise and our desire to praise Him have a totally different motive, both from Him and from us.

What motive is that? It is love and truth, the two absolutely absolute absolutes.

Take *our* motive first. Our love for Him naturally flows over into praise, as does our love for anyone and anything else. If we do not desire to praise Him, we do not love Him much. What idol do you love, and therefore praise, more than God?

As to *His* motive for demanding praise, it is also love, a love that is wholly altruistic, not egotistic; for our sake, not His. "For our sake" means two things: for our joy and for our sanity, for truth. For our second motive for praising Him, after our love, is simply truth: that He is praiseworthy, totally deserving of praise. Praising God is the certification of our sanity, of our conforming our hearts (and therefore our lives, which are always the fruit of our hearts) to objective truth, to the real world, to the nature of things. We need this truth, this conformity to reality absolutely and first of all, so it is for our need, not His, that He commands praise.

Joy is the other thing we need. "Man cannot live without joy", says Saint Thomas. "Therefore when he is deprived of true spiritual joys it is necessary that he become addicted to carnal pleasures." Praising is the natural expression of joy. Praise is joy breathing. That is why Heaven is full of praise.

This psalm is one of the book's two bookends, the other being Psalm 1. The beginning and the end, the alpha and the omega, are one, because it is the very same God that is issuing His fundamental commandment in Psalm 1 and receiving His just praise in Psalm 150.

Psalm 1 told us our fundamental *moral* obligation: to obey, to walk in God's ways. Psalm 150 tells us our fundamental *religious* obligation: to praise. Both obedience and praise are aspects of loving God with our whole heart and soul and mind and strength, which Christ tells us is "the first and great commandment" (Mt 22:38).

This psalm, unlike most of the others, makes only one point. It does not move, so there is no point in tracking its movements. Its last verse repeats its first verse in expanded form—which is what life itself will do for us if we live it God's way: our Heavenly self will be the expanded and perfected version of our earthly self, of our unique and irreplaceable personality and of its unique flourishing and of our unique joy.

> Praise God in his sanctuary:
> praise him in the firmament of his power.

The whole of this little psalm is expansive, inclusive, a "big tent" larger than the universe. This first verse includes both the sacred ("his sanctuary") and the secular ("the firmament of his power", i.e., the universe) and, in doing so, both distinguishes them and unites them: a task our lives and our politics have been struggling with from the beginning.

> Praise him for his mighty acts:
> praise him according to his excellent greatness.

These next two lines include, distinguish, and unite what is external to God, viz., "his mighty acts" in the world, and what is internal to God, "his excellent greatness". We know his internal character from His external acts, as we know each other this way. "His mighty acts" are all acts of love, of salvation, and of revelation. Revelation is what love always does: lovers communicate, sometimes by silence.

Praise him with the sound of the trumpet:
praise him with psaltery and harp.
Praise him with the timbrel and dance:
praise him with stringed instruments and organs.
Praise him upon the loud cymbals:
praise him upon the high sounding cymbals.

These verses list no fewer than nine musical instruments, which stand for the whole panoply of human art and effort: trumpet, psaltery (lute), harp, timbrel (tambourine), dance (which makes a musical instrument out of our bodies), "stringed instruments" (all of them), "organs" (pipes), and both low and high cymbals.

Put these nine instruments together, and you get, not a modern symphony orchestra, but what might be called loud primitive exuberance. You do not get sophisticated modern polyphony. But the essence of music remains unchanged throughout its complex history. In one sense, premodern, "primitive" music was more powerful over human souls than any more advanced modern music, for it so deeply moved ancient cultures like the Jews and, later, the Greeks (there is abundant literary evidence for this) that they spontaneously saw music as a divine gift, a divine inspiration, not merely a human invention. (See Plato's *Ion*, *Republic*, and *Phaedrus* on this. Also read Confucius, who once was so moved by a melody that he could not speak for three days.)

Music and mystical experience are different things and need not happen together. Yet both are modes of consciousness that transcend words. No human art does this better than music, and no human state of consciousness attains it better than mysticism.

Let every thing that hath breath praise the LORD.
Praise ye the LORD.

All the verses in this psalm (in fact, all the "verses" in the "psalm" that is a complete human life) are aspects of the last verse, where the Psalmist calls on absolutely everything that has breath (life) to praise the Lord.

And everything does have breath, everything speaks a word, everything in God's art (i.e., the universe and man and human life) reveals the artist. And if the human artists refuse to sing God's praises, the very rocks will cry out, says Christ, thus showing that "every thing that hath breath" is not confined to literally breathing animals and humans (Lk 19:40).

Because of this, Heaven will not be boring. Nothing interesting, nothing good, and nothing beautiful in the universe will be missing. The only thing that could possibly be missing is you. Make sure you respond to the gracious divine R.S.V.P. to the Universal Cosmic Party. It is even better than "the endless summer" and "the million-year picnic". I hope to see you there.